Focus on JAZZ

Text by
PETER GAMBLE

Photography by
PETER SYMES

St. Martin's Press · New York
Robert Hale · London

Focus on

JAZZ

© Text Peter Gamble 1988
© Photography Peter Symes 1988

ISBN 0-312-02092-9

Library of Congress Cataloging-in-Publication Data

Gamble, Peter.
  Focus on jazz / Peter Gamble : photographs by Peter Symes.
    p.   cm.
  ISBN 0-312-02092-9
  1. Jazz musicians—Portraits   I. Symes, Peter. 1934–
  II. Title.
  ML87.G185 1988
  779′.2′0924—dc19

First edition
10 9 8 7 6 5 4 3 2 1

Robert Hale Limited
Clerkenwell House
Clerkenwell Green
London EC1R 0HT

British Library Cataloguing in Publication Data

Gamble, Peter
    Focus on jazz
    1. Jazz
    I. Title   II. Symes, Peter
    785.42

ISBN 0-7090-3520-9

Typeset in Souvenir Light by
Derek Doyle and Associates, Mold, Clwyd.
Produced in Hong Kong by Bookbuilders Ltd.

Contents

This book is dedicated to
THE MUSICIANS

Foreword

So long as there are jazz musicians, there will be photographers, who love the music, photographing them. Peter Symes is one of these people, and this book is an excellent example of his work in this field.

The musicians who feature within these pages range from 'elder statesmen' to 'the new kid on the block'. Although they are predominantly American, jazz-players of great talent to be found in many countries throughout the world are also introduced.

To cover the entire spectrum of prominent jazz musicians would require a mighty tome indeed but I think the contents of this volume will please the many friends of jazz who find pleasure in the portraiture of great jazz artists.

Introduction
A State of the Art – The Eighties

The development of jazz can be traced along natural evolutionary routes. It has often been blighted by its followers' sectarian fanaticism but, for the practitioners themselves, there have been few insurmountable barriers. Time has continually proved to be a remarkable healer, and jazz, throughout its chequered history, has established a tradition for stylistic co-operation and collective empiricism.

Its story has unfolded at a staggering pace since its earliest days. Fumbling musical illiteracy was rapidly eradicated in the collective skills of the embryonic music. The formalism of ragtime and the stark reality of the blues were just two of the ingredients in a creative melting-pot that finally offered up a music of immeasurable beauty and genuine profundity. The gramophone record began the task of documenting it in 1917, and since then every decade has made its own massive contribution.

To analyse any ten-year period in isolation is to be tempted by certain generalizations. Nevertheless, certain important patterns did emerge in the 1980s, based on the styles that flourished in the fifties and sixties. In some ways, it was a period of consolidation, but it would be something of an over-simplification to see it purely as this. In the broadest sense, jazz in the eighties did temper the incontinent licence claimed by certain of the free-form expressionists; it also muted the volume levels demanded by the extreme fusionists. At the same time, it was a period that encouraged players to regard musical cohesion with less suspicion. There was a greater sense of organization within groups and increasing evidence of players remaining loyal to one unit.

Devices such as the electronic 'freak-out' and the faked contrapuntal all-in suddenly sounded dated and the arranger returned to his rightful status in the jazz world. The music continued to evolve on all fronts, but it was perhaps the rhythm sections that dictated the pace. Rhythmic displacement had always been a finely tuned art, and in the fifties and sixties men like Elvin Jones, Dennis Charles, Ed Blackwell, Milford Graves, Sunny Murray and Beaver Harris had shown how a drummer could be at once supportive yet still highly individualistic. The fragmentation of accent organization could appear, on the surface, to be counterproductive but it became obvious that the horn-players of the era could match the competition and, in fact, be stimulated by it.

Rhythmic shading reached such a degree of subtlety that in some cases the responsibility for hearing the pulse was transferred to the listener. It was a situation that encouraged certain players to take full advantage and to play entirely alone.

Saxophonists such as Steve Lacy, Evan Parker and Lol Coxhill, as well as trombonists such as Paul Rutherford and Albert Mangelsdorff, found it an especially rewarding area of investigation and, unlike Coleman Hawkins and Sonny Rollins, did this not as a one-off experiment but as a policy that used the increased audience awareness to their advantage.

Almost as a reaction to this musical direction, the seventies returned the beat to the rhythm section. 'Rock/jazz fusion' was a term that confused superficial listeners into believing that it was simply a matter of grafting horn lines onto a rock-and-roll base. In fact, it was a much more elaborate interaction of rhythmic needs, one that elevated the position of the 'time-keepers' but also required that the bassist provide the harmonic rest points needed by the improvising soloist. The eighties saw a refinement of that principle. There was a move away from the drummer as the prime power source, and greater emphasis was placed on reciprocal rhythmic feeding. It was as if a whole new generation had suddenly comprehended the 'give-and-take' rhythmic exchanges that had always distinguished Art Blakey's relationship with his own Jazz Messengers and with his bassist in particular.

For the contemporary groups it was something of a gradual process but it was one that, not surprisingly, centred on collective co-operation. It was a classic knock-on situation – as the rhythm teams returned to a policy of greater integration, so the horns found the need to show similar solidarity. Not surprisingly, the same principles applied to some important groups that had been established before the eighties but were still in full operation.

Disappointingly, the *Sun Ra Arkestra* took a reactionary path, and over-emphasis on swing-style arrangements took them to the brink of pedantry. Despite the presence of highly individualistic players such as Lester Bowie, Roscoe Mitchell and Joseph Jarman, the *Art Ensemble of Chicago* showed how to be totally at one, even to the extent of occasionally appearing to be just a rhythm section. Saxophonist Wayne Shorter and keyboard-specialist Joe Zawinul ensured that *Weather Report* showed comparable solidarity, but after a promising start the group drifted out of the scene. *The Crusaders*' collective awareness increased, and the *Jazz Messengers*, while introducing new giants like Wynton and Branford Marsalis, offered what was for many the barometer of total integration. It was left to the Rova Saxophone Quartet, SOS (John Surman, Mike Osborne and Alan Skidmore) and the *World Saxophone Quartet*, with the brilliant skills of Hamiet Bluiett, Julius Hemphill, Oliver Lake and David Murray, to lead the growing army of saxophone groups that worked without a rhythm team.

Trumpeter Miles Davis' reappearance in 1981 was welcomed, but the return to his own highest playing standards was rather more delayed. By the middle eighties, however, he had again established the pattern of his dramatic, electric band. Bob Berg provided the heavy saxophone drapes, while the John Scofield traditions were followed up by Robben Ford. In principle, it was still high-energy funk, but once again Davis had assumed centre-stage with his blinding shafts of colour, and the fusion world was again hanging on his aesthetic coat-tails.

Nevertheless, there were variations on the theme. Leroy Jenkins' *Sting* introduced an element of folkish charm. Ray Anderson's *Slickaphonics* brought buskers' hokum to the club environment, while Ronald Shannon Jackson's *Decoding Society* acknowledged the dance element. Black Arthur Blythe employed star soloists like cellist Abdul Wadud and tuba-specialist Bob Stewart and, with only modest compromise, gained a CBS contract.

The heavy metal/jazz fusion scene was dominated by two Sonny Sharrock groups, *Material* offered a free funk spirit and was the more earthy in its approach, but it was *Last Exit* that made the bigger impact. The leader's blues-drenched guitar found competitive rivalry in the machine-gun-fast tenor of Peter Brötzmann, and their quartet showed that there was still room for unexpected subtleties within the metal/jazz area. The brilliant Ornette Coleman, together with his group, *Prime Time*, progressed along his own harmolodic route to musical monism. In the process, he did not lose contact with the past and, together with trumpeter Don Cherry, bassist Charlie Haden and drummer Billy Higgins, he stunned the 1987 JVC Festival audiences in New York with a highly spectacular reprise of the Atlantic label quartet of the late fifties.

The progress of other free-form pioneers and second-generation revolutionaries was less clear-cut. The brilliance of Cecil Taylor's pianistics shone on the contemporary dance world. Radicals such as Sam Rivers, Chico Freeman and Bobby Hutcherson took more conservative paths, but it was the arch-iconoclast Archie Shepp who changed most drastically. A policy begun in the seventies and continued steadfastly in the eighties saw the tenor saxophonist appointing himself a living legend – a walking, playing history of his chosen instrument who, in performance, portrayed the past as represented by Coleman Hawkins, Ben Webster, Lester Young and John Coltrane.

New faces appeared in the persons of Olu Dara, a trumpeter aware of tradition but very much an original voice. Fellow-trumpeter Terence Blanchard emerged from the *Jazz Messengers* to make his own mark, and young saxophonists such as Eric Persons, Donald Harrison, John Purcell and Steve Coleman impressed strongly. The new breed of trombonists was represented by Craig Harris, Steve Turre and Ray Anderson, while groups such as *Out of the Blue* and *Shadowfax* guaranteed that the 'New Age' was presented by youthful exponents.

The most outstanding of the young reed men was Steve Coleman, an Ornette Coleman disciple who appeared with the very exciting but short-lived *Dave Holland Group*. He was a fine prospect, even if his own group, *Five Elements*, took him rather near to popular compromise. Much the same could be said of John Purcell, another player whose personal skills were given less creative sustenance than they deserved in his own group, *Third Kind of Blue*.

During the eighties, the irreplaceable Count Basie and Woody Herman died, and for many people it really was the end of an era. But former sideman Frank Foster kept the legend alive with an aggregation that still managed to capture much of the Basie slow burn, while Mercer Ellington led an orchestra that presented his father's compositions in a Dukal manner. Unfortunately, both were in the nostalgia market, and it was left to the bands led by David Murray and Olu Dara to show that the larger orchestra could still make a musical comment without perpetuating the old values. They used the vernacular of the free revolution but brought to their music a genuine sense of organization.

Despite this, the constraints on the size of bands did not change. In the main, clubs could afford only smaller units, and it was the quartet and quintet that still cornered the job market. Styles, however, were more varied, and it was groups such as Sirone's *Ensemble* and Billy Bang's brilliant *String Trio of New York* that gave a positive direction to chamber jazz. Fortunately, compromise was always possible, and it was medium-sized groups such as the *David Murray Octet*, Lester Bowie's *Brass Fantasy* and *The George Coleman Octet* that most typified the spirit of the decade. Their work demonstrated how arrangements had again become an important part in a performance; solos were rarely left in limbo, and collective passages displayed far more conscious cohesion. Jazz was acknowledging its past without resorting to plagiarism.

The old traditions remained firmly in the hands of the men who created them. The blues dramatist B.B. King assumed the Muddy Waters crown and became the best-known popularist of his chosen form. Adelaide Hall, the only survivor of Duke Ellington's 1927 Jungle Band, continued to bring her own wistful charm to the same idiom. Joe Turner died but Jimmy Witherspoon and Cleanhead Vinson remained to shout the blues with real conviction. Joe Williams delivered the more calm aspects of the idiom while, in complete contrast, Slim Gaillard moved to London to confound the inhabitants with forties jive and his own special kind of instrumental know-how.

Till his very last day, Freddie Green refused to let the guitar die as a rhythm instrument, while trombonist Al Grey and tenor saxophonist Buddy Tate, former colleagues from *The Count Basie Orchestra*, teamed up to remind the world of the continued potency of the small swing combo. Trumpeter Harry 'Sweets' Edison continued on a solo course of unashamed communication, while giants like Benny Goodman, Zoot Sims, Art Pepper and Sonny Stitt played out their last years with musical dignity and no little excitement.

Lionel Hampton continued to amaze with his brilliant musicianship and indomitable spirit, and the vibraphone's less extrovert persona was presented by Red Norvo in a chamber group that also featured guitarist Tal Farlow. It was perhaps the King, Benny Carter, who most personified the quality of the older traditions. Still playing superbly well on alto saxophone, he continued to win followers to the cause throughout the decade.

Survivors of the forties bebop years continued to flourish. Max Roach led a fine group and, on record, joined forces with a chamber unit to present a novel form of double quartet. The clown prince, Dizzy Gillespie, still played superbly when the mood, the Big Band and the audience were right, and the astylistic Joe Newman continued to deliver his trumpet orations with the lyricism of a poet. The eccentric Tony Scott brought a message of his own to the clarinet, while second-generation giants such as trombonist Slide Hampton and tenor saxophonists Joe Henderson and Johnny Griffin continued to play with real authority – the latter pair in *The* 11

Paris Reunion Band, a group made up of men who had spent more than a little time on the Continent.

The European scene itself continued to flourish. The truly international co-operative aptly named *Company* continued to present its *avant-garde* version of the jam session. The more light-hearted approach was presented by Holland's *Willem Breuker Kollektief*, Italy's *Lingomania* and Scandinavia's *Masqualero*. In Britain, *Loose Tubes* employed more than twenty musicians and introduced a new generation to jazz, while saxophonists such as Courtney Pine and Steve Williamson were prime movers in a British black jazz movement. A large Asian movement was spearheaded by pianist Vyacheslav Ganelin, and his trio actually appeared at the 1987 New York Festival.

On the record front, Concord continued to present the older styles, while CBS and the other majors put their faith in the funk/jazz market. With the enthusiastic Michael Cuscuna's inspiration, there was a revitalization of Blue Note, and it rapidly returned to the label's finest standards. Ironically, it was Italy's Black Saint and its stable-mate Soul Note that continued to provide the true documentation of the black American *avant-garde*. Both labels served the acoustic groups particularly well and genuinely helped to progress the careers of eighties heavyweights such as David Murray, Craig Harris, Billy Bang and the World Saxophone Quartet.

The club-and-concert circuit continued its astylistic ways but, if one single club typified the spirit of the eighties, it was Sweet Basil's: in one single week in 1987 the New York club presented Doc Cheatham, the late Gil Evans and David Murray.

Cheatham is a trumpeter who played soprano saxophone on a 1926 recording by blues legend Ma Rainey. His career traced the journey from the music's early years through to the barnstorming days of the big band era and then beyond to his own small groups of the seventies. Evans, an arranging master inextricably bound up with Miles Davis, showed how his brilliant musical mind could serve almost any stylistic persuasion. In contrast, Murray represented the *avant-garde* but, in so doing, showed how he could use his dazzling skill on tenor saxophone and bass clarinet to bring together the disparate elements that make up jazz's hundred-year history. His big band placed swing-style stalwarts alongside the young tigers of the day; he chose Jelly Roll Morton compositions from the twenties and expressed them through the free vernacular of the present. The outcome was a kaleidoscope of jazz particles that owed allegiance to no single area of the music.

In seven days Sweet Basil's had shown that most jazz styles cohabit with each other naturally and that no assessment of the 'state of the art' is valid without a reference to the past.

Barry McRae

Stanley William (Stan) Tracey OBE   b. Tooting, London, UK,
30 December 1926

On Friday 23 September 1983 a concert was held at London's Queen Elizabeth Hall in celebration of Stan Tracey's forty years in the business. Fittingly the MC was Ronnie Scott, who had employed Stan as his house pianist between 1960 and 1967, shortly after his departure from Ted Heath's band. Invaluable times were those for Stan, backing as he did the cream of jazz talent, including Sonny Rollins and Ben Webster. He formed his first quartet during the Scott residency, with the tenor saxophonist Bobby Wellins, the chosen horn-player, and as a result the richly acclaimed *Under Milk Wood* materialized.

Leaving Scott's, the quartet continued with different personnel, but Stan's interests were broadening, his writing an increasingly important factor as the units he led mushroomed into sextets, octets and big bands. His own record label, STEAM, materialized; he undertook solo concerts and partnered Mike Osborne, John Surman, Keith Tippett and Tony Coe in refreshing duo adventures.

Tracey's major compositions for the octet, *The Bracknell Connection* and *Salisbury Suite*, feature bold themes and bustling solos. *Genesis*, a recent suite for the big band, drew favourable comparisons with Duke Ellington, his guiding light. A very fine tribute to the Duke's music is *Stan Tracey Plays Duke Ellington*, released in 1987, with only bass-player Roy Babbington in support.

Stan Tracey is a glorious institution, father of British contemporary jazz, a pianist capable of great subtlety, despite a naturally percussive inclination, and a composer blessed with flashes of inspired brilliance.

13

Muddy Waters (McKinley Morganfield)   b. Rolling Fork, Mississippi, USA, 4 April 1915, d. 30 April 1983

The late Muddy Waters is the single most important personality of post-war Chicago blues. Raised on a plantation by a grandmother, he was discovered by Alan Lomax on one of his Library of Congress trips and subsequently recorded in 1941. At the time Muddy played and sang in a typical country blues vein, the starting-point for the later-to-be-developed rhythm and blues which so attracted British rock bands in the 1960s. He had a number of hit records in the R'n'B charts including the classic 'Got My Mojo Working' and 'I'm Your Hoochie Coochie Man' which were to become obligatory inclusions in all public performances for the rest of his life. His band's personnel reads like a *Who's Who* of blues artistes: Little Walter Jacobs, Otis Spann, Fred Below, Willie Dixon, Buddy Guy and Junior Wells are just a sample from the roster.

Muddy's fortunes changed dramatically due to bands like the Rolling Stones publicly acknowledging the debt they owed him, and a whole new audience became available to him over the last twenty years of his life, an eventful period in which he survived an almost-fatal car accident and also picked up a couple of Grammy awards. Despite increased popularity and attempts to over-commercialize the genuine product, he never lost that authentic raw quality in his voice allied to that special vibrancy that singled him out as the most exciting of artists.

When McKinley Morganfield died, in 1983, part of the blues tradition died alongside him.

Alexis Korner   b. Paris, France, 19 April 1928, d. 1 January 1984

The death of Alexis Korner in 1984 robbed the blues of a great publicist and no mean performer, while jazz lost a good friend. His initial tentative steps with the Chris Barber band to establish a foothold for blues enthusiasts met only marginal success, and as a direct result *Blue Incorporated* sprang to life, making its first appearance at the Marquee club in 1962. A veritable haven for budding blues purists, future rock superstars and younger jazzmen, Incorporated boasted a fluctuating personnel, led by harmonica-player Cyril Davis and later to include Jack Bruce, Charlie Watts, Mick Jagger, Graham Bond, Long John Baldry, Paul Jones and John Surman.

When the band ceased to exist, Korner first attempted solo work and then formed *New Church* with Danish singer Peter Thorup. Colin Hodgkinson, the bass-player, joined them, he and Korner eventually playing clubs and festivals as a duo. A big band called *CCS*, put together by Korner and featuring his rasping vocals, burned brightly on the pop music front, making the charts and BBC TV's *Top of the Pops*. The rocking surroundings of *Rockett 88* (enter Bruce and Watts once more) suited his needs ideally as the eighties beckoned.

A wonderful broadcaster, his catholic tastes often surprised his most devoted listeners – a Robert Johnson blues was quite likely to butt up against a fairly *avant-garde* jazz piece. Whatever the *genre*, his unbounded enthusiasm, supported by sound critical judgement, earned Korner the respect of his contemporaries.

Doc Cheatham, Benny Carter and Jimmy Maxwell

James Kendrick (Jimmy) Maxwell   b. Stockton, California, USA,
9 January 1917

Organizers and leaders of big bands will tell you that, like good drummers, lead trumpet-players are worth their weight in gold. If this be the case, Jimmy Maxwell should be a rich man, having held down a seat in some of the top sections since his teenage introduction to the first Gil Evans band. Jimmy Dorsey warranted a brief stopover, on Maxwell's way to the Benny Goodman band between 1939 and 1943, his trumpet colleagues including Billy Butterfield, Ziggy Elman and Cootie Williams at one time or another.

Maxwell's big band life subsequently took in Paul Whiteman, Count Basie, Duke Ellington, Quincy Jones, Oliver Nelson, Gerry Mulligan, Lionel Hampton and a Russian tour for Goodman. Leonard Feather tells of his recording with John Lennon and playing the bagpipes in New York's St Patrick's Day Parade. The soundtrack of *The Godfather* features the Maxwell trumpet.

A horn-player with a sharp tone, clarity of purpose and vigorous attack.

Adolphus Anthony (Doc) Cheatham   b. Nashville, Tennessee, USA, 13 June 1905

'Doc's' history goes back to the days of vaudeville and the burlesque shows. In the 1930s he plied his trade in the bands of Marion Hardy, Teddy Wilson, Cab Calloway and Benny Carter, also spending a period as a constituent part of *McKinney's Cotton Pickers*. Such diverse talents as Billie Holliday, Machito, Ma Rainey and Shorty Baker have benefited from the Cheatham horn being in attendance.

To the present day the trumpeter's pedigree has allowed him to work on a regular basis, including a stint with Benny Goodman in 1967. He is a much under-rated musician throughout a good percentage of jazz history, who is equally at home leading a section or taking a solo. Much travelled and highly respected.

Bennett Lester (Benny) Carter   b. New York City, USA, 8 August 1907

As one of the outstanding figures of jazz history, multi-instrumentalist Carter is often mentioned in the same breath as Johnny Hodges when the important influences of the alto saxophone are discussed. In the late twenties and early thirties, his apprenticeship years were spent in the bands of Fletcher Henderson, Chick Webb and Charlie Johnson. During that time he taught himself the rudiments of arranging, opening up the opportunity to take over the musical directorship of *McKinney's Cotton Pickers* in 1931. Spending time in Europe from 1935 to 1938, he arrived in London to become the staff arranger for the popular *Henry Hall Orchestra* before a return to the States, where he formed a well-respected big band.

Since the mid forties Carter has lived in Hollywood, writing scores for both films and television programmes, although jazz never lost him totally to the lure of tinsel town. Now over eighty years of age, he is still known to play in public. His alto-playing is blessed by a liquid tone that is never put to better effect than on a good melody that encourages graceful, clean lines, a Carter trademark. When all aspects of the man's talent are weighed up – and this must include his marvellous instinct for saxophone arrangements, the word 'quality' could not be bettered.

Louis T. Moholo   b. Cape Town, South Africa. 10 March 1940

With Louis Moholo in the driving seat, no band could complain that their music lacked impetus. There is a raw, intuitive spontaneity in the manner in which he navigates the drum kit that couldn't possibly be achieved from months of tuition. As a time-keeper he is superb, and when thrust into group improvisation, the drummer is never found wanting.

No sooner had he arrived in the UK than off to South America he went with Steve Lacy, to return and demonstrate his exploding power in Europe. Many bands have welcomed his presence, *Brotherhood of Breath*, the *Mike Osborne Trio* and *Elton Dean's Ninesense* among them. Pianist Keith Tippett partnered him in a duo, recording in Berlin and appearing at the 1982 Bracknell Festival. Moholo sat in Tippett's mammoth big band *Ark*, performed in a percussion duet with American Andrew Cyrille and led a number of bands of his own, *Spirits Rejoice*, *Viva La Black* and *The African Drum Ensemble* being the better known. *Spirits Rejoice* are featured on an album of the same name, made in 1978 and characterized by the invigorating music generic to the drummer's personality.

Johnny Dyani   b. East London, South Africa, 30 November 1945,
d. 27 October 1986

Dyani arrived in Britain in 1965 at the end of a European tour by the South African band *Blue Notes*, led by pianist Chris McGregor and completed by Dyani, Dudu Pukwana, Mongezi Feza and Louis Moholo, all of whom were to remain resident in London and make a resounding impact on a then relatively stagnant British scene.

Dyani soon took off on his travels again, and 1966 found him in South America broadening his outlook in a quartet made up by Moholo, Steve Lacy and Enrico Rava. Back in Britain, he put his energies into the *Spontaneous Music Ensemble* and the *Musicians' Co-op*. Taking up residence in Denmark, he blossomed due to his labours with John Tchicai, Don Cherry and fellow South African Abdullah Ibrahim. In 1977 his attendance at a *Brotherhood of Breath* concert in Toulouse was recorded on *Procession*, reunited with his Blue Note colleagues. *Song For Biko*, partnering Pukwana and Cherry a year later, also serves as a fitting legacy.

Although Johnny Dyani sought out the company of free improvisers, the importance of the retention of his folk roots determined the musical directions he took. A masterful and imaginative bass-player who died at a relatively young age in 1986.

Chris McGregor   b. Somerset West, South Africa, 24 December 1936

On 27 June 1970 a big band under the leadership of Chris McGregor took the stage of London's Notre Dame Hall. Known from then on as The *Brotherhood of Breath*, they took the club scene by storm, centred on the piano of the leader and other members of the *Blue Notes* who had arrived in Britain in 1965. The infectious concoction of township music, collective free-for-alls and driving unison passages captured the imagination of a large following who religiously turned out at each gig. They were far and away the most exciting prospect then resident on the British circuit.

McGregor continued working with the *Blue Notes* and the *Brotherhood* until he moved to France in the mid seventies. His piano-playing is frequently heard at festivals in Europe, sometime solo, often within a small group and just occasionally when he is tempted to resurrect the *Brotherhood*. Unfortunately, as with most re-creations, the spirit and joy of the original band have never been quite recaptured.

The pianist and composer has always been a popular figure on the international jazz scene, his keyboard endeavours consistently praised, but for those of us lucky enough to remember the heady days of the early seventies, Chris McGregor's name will always be synonymous with the *Brotherhood of Breath*.

Cecil Percival Taylor   b. New York City, USA; 15 March 1933

There are few more controversial figures in jazz than Cecil Taylor, the pianist/composer who could have invented the word 'uncompromising' with his resolute belief in the totally improvised and his complete rejection of anything smacking of harmony or melody in the conventional sense. His attacks on the keyboard, for that is what they are, constitute an endurance test for both himself and the listener. Detractors have declared him 'non-jazz' and tedious; supporters revel in the stimulation the inspired improviser can offer them. The two-handed assault he employs produces heavily percussive sequences of densely packed clusters, building upon each other to create a rainbow effect quite unlike anything jazz has experienced before.

Taylor's beginnings were relatively staid; training at a conservatoire, playing with Johnny Hodges and Lawrence Brown. However, the middle to late fifties were responsible for the transformation of the pianist into the figure we know today. Leading groups including Steve Lacy, Buell Neidlinger, Earl Griffith and Dennis Charles, his style slowly drifted into unexplored territory, maturing further as he spent a good few months in Europe, recording at Copenhagen's Café Montmartre with Jimmy Lyons and Sunny Murray; Albert Ayler also became a workmate for a period. Taylor recorded with *The Jazz Composers Orchestra* and formed a working band which alienated a few outraged customers at Jazz Expo 69. Sam Rivers left the band in 1973 but Lyons, supported by Andrew Cyrille, stayed in the pianist's charge for much longer.

At the Montreux Festival in 1974, Taylor appeared as a solo act, increasingly wishing to do so, and the results are available on the devastatingly brilliant *Silent Tongues*. Three years on, Carnegie Hall was the setting for a shared concert with veteran pianist Mary Lou Williams. However, the duet confrontations harnessed to drummer Max Roach are manifestly more demanding and relevant.

Taylor stands as the man who withstood scorn and ridicule to persuade the doubters of his intentions to accept him on his own terms, come what may.

James Stanley (Jim) Hall   b. Buffalo, New York, USA, 4 or 12 December 1930

Jim Hall represents the epitome of tasteful, thoughtful and imaginative guitar-playing. His technical command is second to none, affording him the luxury of studio work, as and when he requires it, and the more demanding milieu of improvised music.

In many respects much of his best playing has come from the duo format; in meetings with Bob Brookmeyer, Bill Evans and Ron Carter the results are notable triumphs for empathy and logic.

Numbered among the noteworthy records Hall has enhanced are: *Jazz Abstractions*, to which he contributed also as a composer; *The Bridge*, from a short stay with Sonny Rollins; *All Night Sessions*, the famous nocturnal sides under Hampton Hawes' name, and *Undercurrent*, a wonderful interactive date with Bill Evans. Gerry Mulligan, George Shearing and Ella Fitzgerald have also claimed him for recordings.

In 1987 the grand surroundings of Bath's Guildhall staged a resurrection of the Brookmeyer connection, the valve trombone and guitar tracing intricate patterns around a hatful of standard tunes and original compositions – Brookmeyer hesitant at times, Hall plugging the gaps and brimming over with ideas.

Robert (Bob) Brookmeyer   b. Kansas City, Kansas, USA, 19 December 1929

Best known as a valve trombonist, Brookmeyer in fact started as a pianist in the big bands of Woody Herman and Claude Thornhill. However, when he joined Stan Getz in 1953, the trombone had overtaken the keyboard as his main instrument. Completing a double tour of duty with Gerry Mulligan, he made a move to complete the *Jimmy Giuffre Trio* with Jim Hall, then worked around New York for a number of different leaders, ending up in 1960 in the *Gerry Mulligan Band* again.

Brookmeyer's writing and arranging abilities found an outlet in the New York Studios and with the *Thad Jones-Mel Lewis Orchestra*, a working showcase until 1968, when Los Angeles became his base and the TV studios the medium into which his energies were channelled, with the odd respite in Jones-Lewis and Mulligan re-unions. His eventual return to New York a good ten years later allowed him to renew old acquaintances and re-establish his name on the jazz scene.

Many people have made the observation that Brookmeyer's playing – and, by extension, composing/arranging – has a cold, clinical aspect. This is occasionally true, maybe, but one can never ignore the all-round talent of one such as he: as a writer he warrants respect, as a musician his consistently agile horn-playing demands attention.

Abbey Lincoln (Aminata Moseka)   b. Chicago, Illinois, USA, 6 August 1930

Singer Abbey Lincoln had been regarded as a cabaret-type performer before falling under the spell of drummer Max Roach. Although Benny Carter and Thelonious Monk could be listed amongst her backing musicians, it was only when she entered into working and matrimonial partnership with Roach that she found her true voice.

With a passionate delivery, half sung, half spoken, she graced *We Insist: Freedom Now Suite, Percussion Bitter Sweet* and *Straight Ahead* in a manner moving in its intensity and commitment, compared by many to Billie Holiday.

Her acting, running in parallel to the singing, finally peaked when she starred in the 1968 film *For Love of Ivy*, but her marriage to Roach floundered. Lincoln continues her dual vocations but keeps a low profile in jazz terms – a great pity for anyone who is aware of her previous triumphs.

Maxwell (Max) Roach   b. Brooklyn, New York, USA, 10 January 1925

Indisputably one of the finest of all modern drummers, Roach has exercised an influence over countless percussionists for a period of forty years. Inspired by Kenny Clarke, he spent the revolutionary days between 1946 and 1948 as Charlie Parker's driving force, turning jazz drumming upside down. The emphasis of the beat moved to the cymbal and allowed the drummer a much freer role within the overall group context.

In 1954 he formed a classic quintet including trumpeter Clifford Brown and tenor-players Harold Land and Sonny Rollins, sadly terminated by the death of Brown and pianist Richie Powell in a car crash. The brilliant young Booker Little, also a trumpeter destined for an early demise, joined Roach in 1958 to form another fine band. Always a campaigner for black equality, the drummer's known activities and attitudes earned him a five-year ban from the recording studios. The *Freedom Now Suite*, from 1960, employing the then Mrs Roach, singer Abbey Lincoln, is a heartfelt protest document.

In recent times Roach has continued to lead a regular quartet, featuring trumpeter Cecil Bridgewater and tenor-player Odean Pope, an ensemble that frequently collaborates successfully with a string quartet that includes the drummer's daughter. The percussion group *M'Boom* is also a project high in priority, although Roach's meeting in a concert setting with the iconoclastic pianist Cecil Taylor would be hard to match in creative terms. He rightly commands much respect by all involved in the music and is very much aware of his status.

Ian Ernest Gilmore Green (Gil) Evans   b. Toronto, Canada, 13 May 1912, d. 20 March 1988

The *Claude Thornhill Orchestra* of the forties featured arrangements from two jazzmen destined to make substantial contributions to the music over the next forty years: the first was Gerry Mulligan, the second Gil Evans. The Evans touch on ballads and bop tunes can be easily singled out from records available from the period, and we hear the clever scoring for French horns blending with the tuba that featured strongly in much of his later arranging.

Only in 1952 did he commence playing piano in public but, like Duke Ellington's philosophy, Evans' instrument will forever be his orchestra, never more apparent than in the collaboration with Miles Davis which produced recorded masterpieces *Porgy and Bess, Sketches of Spain* and *Miles Ahead.* One of the highlights of the *Sketches* album was Rodrigo's *Concierto de Aranjuez*, a magnificent live performance of which has only just been released, it having come from the Carnegie Hall concert of 1961. About the same time Gil's orchestra presented *Out of the Cool*, a most imaginative and interesting collection.

The sixties were low on Evans appearances but the early seventies heralded a new era. He had absorbed much of the language of rock music into his thinking, and the 1974 *Music of Jimi Hendrix* gave proof positive of a refusal to be left in the past. His first British concert was given at the Festival Hall in 1978, leading a band packed solid with big names – David Sanborn, Ernie Royal, Arthur Blythe, George Adams and Bob Stewart, to name but a few. The results from this date were electrifying. Back he came in 1983, fronting a British band that spluttered slightly at London's Roundhouse; he recorded to better effect in Bradford but roared magnificently when taken into Ronnie Scott's at a much later date.

Though past his seventy-fifth birthday, Evans still led a regular band at Sweet Basil's and chose to travel to the major festivals, a remarkable testimony to the importance of the composer/arranger in the province of essentially improvised music. He was planning another trip to Britain when he died in March 1988.

George Rufus Adams   b. Covington, Georgia, USA, 29 April 1940

Tenor saxophonist Adams emerged from a background in the Church to spend his instructional years in R'n'B bands, a grounding that was to manifest itself in later work for the bands of Art Blakey and Charles Mingus. He has piloted bands of his own but is best known for his long-standing relationship with Gil Evans, plus a successful quartet led jointly with ex-Mingus pianist Don Pullen. The quartet is exceptionally well captured on a series of exciting albums that catch the group in both live and studio settings.

The uncompromising, bold and aggressive approach that Adams adopts is instantly recognizable and, if there is a periodic tendency in solos to fall back on a clutch of well-worn clichés, this can be easily forgiven in the face of the musician's natural, effervescent exuberance. For one whose abrasive style singles him out, he is still capable of bringing the most sympathetic of natures to bear on the tenderest of ballads.

He is equally popular on both sides of the Atlantic, and there is a constant air of expectation when George Adams takes to the bandstand, and if the growling blues vocals he enjoys performing are an acquired taste, the booting tenor excursion to follow rarely disappoints the audience.

Michael John David (Mike) Westbrook b. High Wycombe, Buckinghamshire, UK, 21 March 1936 and **Kate Westbrook** b. Guildford, Surrey, UK

Mike Westbrook descended on London in 1962 and quickly drew attention to his sextet, including John Surman. His writing being of paramount importance urged him to form a larger ensemble, in the *Mike Westbrook Concert Band*, a talented big band populated by Malcolm Griffiths, Paul Rutherford, Mike Osborne, Surman and other front-line modernists. *Celebration, Marching Song* and *Metropolis* all do justice to the refreshing Westbrook compositions and the power of the band.

Solid Gold Cadillac replaced the *Concert Band* as Mike's means of expression in 1971, leaning very definitely in the direction of rock music, but the *Brass Band* rapidly replaced *Cadillac*. It was the first Westbrook group to show signs of Mike's growing interest in non-jazz works and multi-media presentations. Kate joined forces with him at this juncture and produced the 1975 *Citadel/Room 315* album, a re-formation of the orchestra, John Surman taking the majority of solos.

The arrival of Kate, singer and tenor horn-player, led Mike to an even smaller line-up, a trio called *A Little Westbrook Music*, ironically formed in 1982, the year of another major work, *Bright as Fire*. This was based on the poems of William Blake and heavily featured the voices of Kate and Phil Minton. Three years on and *On Duke's Birthday* received as much critical acclaim as had the ambitious Blake project before it.

Mike's earliest influences, firmly cast in the jazz mould, disappeared long ago and, with Kate established firmly as his sympathetic partner, there is no telling which direction the pair may turn in next.

Paul William Rutherford   b. Greenwich, London, UK, 29 February 1940

One of the leading members of the European 'Free' school, Rutherford stands alongside Albert Mangelsdorff and Gunter Christmann as one of today's truly gifted and innovative trombonists. His career started fortuitously: having met like-minded individuals John Stevens and Trevor Watts in the RAF, he was to join them in the experimental *Spontaneous Musical Ensemble*, a band that became a proving-ground for many a talented musician. The experience he gained in the *Mike Westbrook Orchestra* did him no harm, the trombonist really blossomed when allowed to express himself within the context of bands like the *Tony Oxley Sextet, The London Jazz Composers Orchestra, Iskra 1903* and the multi-national *Globe Unity Orchestra*, all devoted to free improvisation on a most committed scale – although that is not to say that the more conventional aspects of contemporary music are totally alien to him.

Perhaps the current trio, with Paul Rogers on bass and Nigel Morris taking care of percussion, is the most suitable framework in which to appreciate Rutherford's talents. A tape, recently released, of the band's fine performance at the 1983 Bracknell Jazz Festival features the leader in just the kind of form that moved the respected American critic John Litweiler to remark in his book *The Freedom Principle* that Rutherford displays 'the very soul of unreason' – intended, of course, as the highest compliment.

**Evan
Shaw
Parker**
b. Bristol, UK,
5 April 1944

Few musicians can boast a technique as awesome as Evan Parker's. His matchless command of both the soprano and tenor saxophones could be enough to frighten away any potential newcomers to the playing of reed instruments, able comfortably to descend or ascend beyond the natural ranges prescribed by the accepted norm. With the aid of circular breathing, he is capable of stringing out long, intricate and convoluted lines without seeming to flag either cerebrally or physically. His chosen niche takes him far beyond the approved rules of melody and harmony, as he invariably finds himself pushing out the barriers, amongst the cream of Europe's 'free' academy or experimenting as a solo artist.

When Parker moved to London in the early sixties and almost immediately involved himself with John Stevens' *Spontaneous Music Ensemble*, he could have little realized that the experience would set him firmly on the road leading to the *Musicians' Co-Operative* and the *Globe Unity Orchestra*, organized by musicians of a similar persuasion.

In mid-February 1988 Parker could be found pursuing a Contemporary Music Network tour in conjunction with the Dutch collective known as the *Instant Composers Pool*, as apt a piece of programming as one could find. Reviewers were strong in their praise for Parker's continued pathfinding and his seemingly inexhaustible searching for further extensions to the language of the saxophone.

Alvin Gilbert (Al) Cohn   b. Brooklyn, New York, USA, 24 November 1925, d. 16 February 1988

The tenor saxophonist Al Cohn spent much time in various big bands of the forties, including those of Artie Shaw and Woody Herman, replacing one of the original 'Four Brothers', Herbie Steward, when joining the ranks of the Herman Herd. The two-tenor partnership of himself and the late Zoot Sims turned out to be a popular success in the fifties, the pair having contrasted approaches in phrasing and attack, enabling the music to retain a certain variety and degree of surprise. Being an accomplished arranger, he often disappeared from the performing world for lengthy stretches, writing for TV shows and Broadway musicals.

His son Joe is a talented guitarist, and the two generations often combined together in melodic harmony. Cohn senior had a number of releases under his name for the Concord record label, and *Standards Of Excellence* captures him in a wholly satisfying context, relaxed and niftily negotiating some tried and trusted old war-horses. Al Cohn died in February 1988.

John Haley (Zoot) Sims   b. Inglewood, California, USA, 29 October 1925,
d. 23 March 1985

As a teenager Zoot Sims joined the band of Bobby Sherwood; he gravitated to
Benny Goodman and in 1947 secured a place in history as one of Woody
Herman's Four Brothers saxophone section, alongside Stan Getz, Herbie Steward
and Serge Chaloff. Two years with Herman set him on the road to associations
with Artie Shaw, Al Cohn, in a two-tenor partnership, and Gerry Mulligan's Sextet,
who toured Europe sporting a front line completed by John Eardley and Bob
Brookmeyer.

He frequently returned to the Goodman fold but up to his death in 1985 more
often than not liked to work under his own name, in front of local rhythm sections
or specially assembled groups or as a guest artist.

Many recordings are available that portray the essence of Sims the craftsman:
the Pablo creations *If I'm Lucky* (1977) and *Quietly There* (1984) broadly
encapsulate the saxophonist's playing ethic. One of a whole army of tenorists
influenced by Lester Young, he and Stan Getz were the individuals who
embellished the basic Young ideals with their original innovations, formulating two
distinct strains. Sims had a strong melodic feel that operated very much on the
principle 'It isn't so much what you play but how you play it.' He played it
perfectly!

Stanley Jordan   b. Chicago, Illinois, USA, 31 July 1959

Guitarist Stanley Jordan is a very recent phenomenon, taken from relative obscurity and thrust into the limelight at the 1984 Kool Jazz Festival. The fascination he commands is due to a unique technique of tapping the strings with both hands rather than plucking them. He has been marketed very successfully and is extremely popular on the international circuit.

Two albums on the Blue Note record lable, *Magic Touch* from 1984 and *Standards, Vol. I* two years later are perfect examples of what one might expect from Jordan in concert.

Perhaps the most perfect summing-up of Jordan was made in 1987 by journalist and guitarist Mark Gilbert: 'Contentwise, he simply reiterates modern jazz guitar style, though not as fluently as a duet of Barney Kessel and John McLaughlin might.' The world waits for the real Stanley Jordan to stand up.

Billy Bang (Billy Walker)   b. Mobile, Alabama, USA, 20 September 1947

The number of important violinists contributing to the history of jazz is very small indeed. The significant roster will always include Joe Venuti, Stephane Grappelli, Eddie South and Stuff Smith, the modernists being represented by Jean-Luc Ponty, Leroy Jenkins, the dabblings of Ornette Coleman and finally Billy Bang. Tutored by Jenkins but sporting the earthy, more blues-orientated qualities of Smith, Bang is the premier violinist of his day.

The meaningful appearances of the *String Trio of New York* were a significant proving-ground, but he is probably better known on a wider basis for the groups he has led, including firstly Charles Tyler on saxophones and latterly tenor man Frank Lowe. The band featuring Lowe and his long-time favourite drummer Dennis Charles is entitled *The Jazz Doctors*, hence performances require the wearing of appropriate white coats. The album *Intensive Care* can be put down as one of their most successful operations.

In 1987 Bang made several guest appearances, none more exotic than the one with the *Sun Ra Arkestra* at New York's JVC Festival, when the bedecked throng appeared in Central Park. Another significant move of the year was the formation of a trio completed by bass-player Sirone and a Japanese drummer, which took its first public engagement in Greenwich Village. It is reported that the music leaned heavily in the direction of the defunct *Revolutionary Ensemble*, a band of similar instrumentation.

Dennis Charles   b. St Croix, Virgin Islands, 4 December 1933

At the age of eleven Charles moved to New York in the company of his mother. He absorbed the many sounds to be digested in the metropolis and taught himself the basic skills of jazz drumming.

In the fifties emergent innovators Cecil Taylor, Steve Lacy and Jimmy Giuffre took him into their world, and quickly he learnt that there was more to playing the drums than pure time-keeping. Recorded evidence (Cecil Taylor's *Looking Ahead!* and *The World of Cecil Taylor*) indicates an awareness of the greater demands being made on the drummer thirty years ago.

An addiction to heroin and personal family tragedy sadly overtook Charles in 1963, heralding a ten-year absence from the playing arena. The recent past has found him affiliating with violinist Billy Bang, tenor man Frank Lowe and bass-player Raphael Garrett in *The Jazz Doctors*, apparently sound of mind and body.

William Franklin (Bill) Hardman Jnr.   b. Cleveland, Ohio, USA, 6 April 1933

Trumpeter Bill Hardman is inescapably associated with Art Blakey, spending four separate stints in the Messengers, the first in the fifties and the last in the mid seventies. Apart from the Messengers, his early career took shape in the groups of Horace Silver and Charles Mingus and in a partnership with Lou Donaldson lasting from 1959 to 1966.

Several records from the time indicate the flowering potential, not least *The Messengers Meet Thelonious Monk* confrontation on which the trumpet, inspired by Clifford Brown, more than holds its own despite the attentions of probing keyboard and surging tenor supplied courtesy of Johnny Griffin. In 1973 Hardman won the Downbeat Critics Poll, 'Trumpet Deserving Wider Recognition' section, went on to lead *Brass Company* and teamed up with Junior Cook, to acclaim on the touring circuit. Muse record company released examples of the Hardman/Cook success.

William Godvin (Beaver) Harris   b. Pittsburg, Pennsylvania, USA, 20 April 1936

When joining the Archie Shepp band in 1966, Beaver Harris must have been grateful for the experience already under his belt from playing with giants Sonny Rollins and Thelonious Monk. He toured Europe with Shepp, meeting that other *enfant terrible* of the 'new music', Albert Ayler, and subsequently recorded (under the leadership of the turbulent tenor twins) *Mama Too Tight*, Shepp's chaotic but heady mixture of R'n'B, brass band simulation and free improvisation, and *Albert Ayler in Greenwich Village* a typically bold statement from Ayler using alto and tenor saxophones.

Harris continued to keep company with progenitors of the new sounds Roswell Rudd, Marion Brown and Grachan Moncur, with whom he formed a long-standing group, *360 Degree Experience*. As the members of the sixties *avant-garde* mellowed, Harris was backing Shepp in his new guise as a hard bopper and taking to the studio with singer Maxine Sullivan and trumpeter Doc Cheatham. His *In Sanity* on Black Saint produced approving critical voices, as did *Trickles*, a date for the same label, led by Steve Lacy, featuring the drummer and Roswell Rudd. Of late, Harris has given us *French Horn Connection* at the 1985 Camden Festival, Vincent Chauncey, Sam Rivers and Dave Burrell as main soloists, plus a quartet with saxophonist Gijs Hendricks.

Harris is an extremely flexible drummer, whose rhythmic imagination and impeccable time-keeping single him out as a compatible interpreter across a wide spectrum.

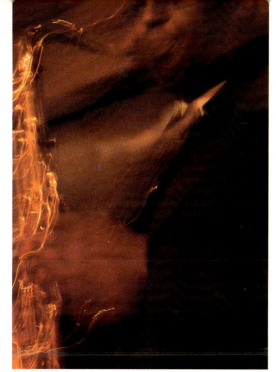

**Archie
Shepp**
b. Fort Lauderdale,
Florida, USA,
24 May 1937

Archie Shepp clearly stood in the vanguard of the 'new music' movement of the sixties, initially tangling manfully with Cecil Taylor, which propelled him into leading a quartet with trumpeter Bill Dixon and formation of the *New York Contemporary Five*, the other hornmen being Don Cherry and John Tchicai.

In 1965 John Coltrane recorded his epic collective *tour de force, Ascension,* Shepp amongst the personnel, and at the Newport Festival of the same year the saxophonists were sharing billing at the head of their respective groups. *New Thing at Newport* reveals the results.

Shepp, now well established, continued to play music reflective of the 'black consciousness' ethic prevalent at the time, the tenor saxophone wielded in protest, alternately bleating, braying, cajoling and pleading. Even so, he never quite managed to disguise his underlying romanticism and, amidst the anger, Ellington's *Prelude to a Kiss* or the unlikely *Girl from Ipanema* might emerge. Albums *On This Night, Fire Music, Mama Too Tight* and *Three for a Quarter, One for a Dime,* with Roswell Rudd, Beaver Harris, Grachan Moncur, Bobby Hutcherson and Joe Chambers, indicate consummately the *modus operandi* employed. An unusual encounter occurred in Paris, released under the title *Black Gipsy,* when Shepp used soprano supported by a personnel including vocalist Chicago Beauchamp, harmonica-player Julio Finn and Leroy Jenkins on viola.

In the middle seventies indications pointed to a changed man, at least in the musical sense. The bellicose warrior now favoured a hard bop stance, and more ballads and standards littered his repertoire. He progressed to recording Sidney Bechet material, a piano album and a tribute to Charlie Parker.

Admirers of the younger Shepp still shake their heads in disbelief at the later model but he was making a statement for an era long past; his current values represent the demands of a different climate. He always stood proud for the rights of the black community and, unlike his music, that will never alter.

Mike Osborne and Alan Skidmore

Michael Evans (Mike) Osborne   b. Hereford, UK, 28 September 1941

Reviewing a Stan Tracey/Mike Osborne recording of 1976, entitled *Tandem*, Barry Mcrae declared the album 'an impressive achievement by any standards' – the sort of comment Mike Osborne received regularly, whether in reference to his recorded work or live performances. Sadly, 'the finest alto in Europe' has had a career blighted by hospitalization, since 1980 his horn has remained silent.

Stan Tracey was a fine partner for Osborne, the *Tandem* album bearing that out, but much of his finest work is considered to have been with the trio completed by Harry Miller and Louis Moholo. *SOS*, the saxophone trio, introduced another platform to stretch out on, the *Mike Westbrook Concert Band* and *Brotherhood of Breath* offering the chance of big band exposure.

Mike listened to the main men – Jackie Mclean, Eric Dolphy and Ornette Coleman, knitted their influences together and manufactured a coat of many colours, only to be worn personally.

Alan Richard James Skidmore   b. Kingston-on-Thames, Surrey, UK, 21 April 1942

Very much in the same way that Von Freeman influenced his son Chico's future, Alan Skidmore must have received considerable direction from tenor-playing father Jimmy, a full-toned reed man of whom too little has been heard of late. However, the family flag flies proudly in the grasp of Alan, long recognized as one of Britain's best saxophonists.

Most of his time in recent years has been spent abroad, touring and playing in Europe and even farther afield, in Asia. *SOH*, the trio with Tony Oxley and Ali

46

Haurand, toured the Continent extensively. His commitment to the *West German Radio Orchestra* for four years also meant absence from his home base for a while. Even so, Skiddy often plays in the *Stan Tracey Big Band*, and it's not that long since he co-led *Tenor Tonic* with Paul Dunmall, a vibrant combination of two tenors ably assisted by bassist Paul Rogers and drummer Tony Levin.

If we cast our eyes back further, Skidmore's colourful pallet would paint a picture of workmates including Alexis Korner, Ronnie Scott, Georgie Fame, Mike Westbrook, Mike Osborne and John Surman.

John Douglas Surman　b. Tavistock, Devon, UK, 30 April 1944

A British saxophonist of true international standing, Surman is regarded by many critics as the finest ever exponent of the baritone. An individual who, alongside Hamiet Bluiett, blew away once and for all, the elephantine connotations attached to the larger horn, he displays a remarkable agility and range few saxophonists have achieved, an ability he can transfer to either bass clarinet or soprano. A creative musician of the very highest order.

After ten years in the *Mike Westbrook Band* and as a component part of many other home-grown groups, Surman led *The Trio* featuring Americans Stu Martin (drums) and Barre Phillips (bass), followed by *SOS* another trio, completed by fellow reed-players Alan Skidmore and Mike Osborne. Both bands represented the very best of what has become loosely referred to as 'free' music.

Working purely as a soloist accompanied only by prepared synthesizers proved to be an enlightening diversion which preceded his currently successful partnership with Norwegian singer Karin Krog. Of late, his appearances in the UK have been limited, due to a constant demand for his services worldwide.

Woody Shaw   b. Laurinburg, North Carolina, USA, 24 December 1944

The sparkling and imaginative trumpet-playing of Woody Shaw has long been held in high regard by his peers, Dizzy Gillespie and Miles Davis heading the list of admirers.

Despite being born in North Carolina, Woody was brought up in New Jersey, where his father belonged to a gospel group, *The Jubilee Singers*. His own playing first received public exposure with organist Larry Young and tenor-player Tyrone Washington. In Paris he played with Kenny Clarke, Bud Powell and Larry Young, with whom he toured the Continent.

Stateside in 1965 Shaw followed Carmell Jones into the Horace Silver group for about a year, superseded by a number of years of patchy employment with McCoy Tyner, Max Roach and Gil Evans. 1973 arrived and he became a Jazz Messenger for a while. Leading his own groups, his fortunes changed, and from 1975 onwards his undeniable talents started to receive their due recognition.

In February 1985 Shaw led an all-star band at the Rebirth of Blue Note concert in New York, featuring Jackie McLean, McCoy Tyner, Cecil McBee and Jack DeJohnette. The same year he arrived in Britain for both the Camden Festival and the Pendley event, taking part at the latter with the *Paris Reunion Band*, who performed the storming set of the festival.

James Bryant (Jimmy) Woode   b. Philadelphia, Pennsylvania, USA, 23 September 1928 or 1929

Jimmy Woode had spent most of his time playing in the environs of Boston when his then employer, George Wein, recommended him to Duke Ellington. His five-year tenure with the band coincided with a resurrection of public interest in the great bandleader/composer, particularly after his triumphant 1956 Newport Festival appearance.

Leaving Duke after five years, Woode made for Europe, working in various countries and making a home in both Germany and Austria. He currently lives in Switzerland. His movement around the Continent has at various times brought him into contact with Dexter Gordon, Ben Webster, Bud Powell, Arnett Cobb, Eddie 'Lockjaw' Davis and Johnny Griffin. He was a regular member of the *Kenny Clarke-Francy Boland Big Band* and is currently part of the *Paris Reunion Band*.

Woode belongs to a distinguished body of bass-players who would be deemed an asset to any rhythm section.

49

Nathan Tate Davis   b. Kansas City, Kansas, USA, 15 February 1937

Lost to the academic world for many years, Davis re-emerged in 1985 as nominal leader of the *Paris Reunion Band*, causing quite a stir at the time, pinning back the ears of a new audience discovering his accomplished tenor and soprano deliberations for the first time.

As a teenager Davis had taken a job offered by Jay McShann which preceded a period of study culminating in an army call-up that took him to Europe, where he stayed after being demobbed and gigged around in the company of name players like Eric Dolphy, Donald Byrd and Kenny Clarke. He returned to the States in 1969 to take up a teaching post at the University of Pittsburg, where he holds down a professorship at present.

Although not recorded substantially, Davis can be heard on the Paris Reunion's *French Cooking* album and a re-release from 1967, *Rules of Freedom*, where the rest of the band is made up by Hampton Hawes, Jimmy Garrison and Art Taylor. This second record featured in the top ten reissues of 1987 when the *Jazz Journal International* critics' poll was published.

**Joseph A. (Joe)
Henderson**
b. Lima, Ohio,
USA, 24 April 1937

Jazz, like any art form, is littered with many practitioners either undervalued or underrated in their lifetime. A suitable case for inclusion could be Joe Henderson, a tenor-player out of the very top drawer, consistently original and almost incapable of giving less than his best. He is unfairly locked into the Coltrane school: his improvisations carry a personal stamp that may flirt in the direction of the master but which end up as pure Henderson. The phraseology depends on quick-witted twists and turns, unusual accents and a determination to let matters unfold logically, rather than going for broke every time he confronts the microphone.

A stalwart from the modern jazz of the sixties, the saxophonist did time in the bands of Kenny Dorham, Horace Silver and Herbie Hancock, then struck out alone for a handful of years. He even lingered for a while amidst the jazz-rock atmosphere of *Blood, Sweat and Tears*. Taking himself off to the West Coast, he continued to perform regularly but also began teaching in a number of colleges, and tours were undertaken on a regular basis.

In the eighties more recognition started to come Henderson's way. In 1986, for example, he twice appeared at Ronnie Scott's in London, once in a quartet format that gave many a patron something to think about, and secondly filling out the *Paris Reunion Band*, his solos far and away the most absorbing and stimulating.

Miles Dewey Davis   b. Alton, Illinois, USA, 25 May 1926

Unarguably one of jazz's living legends, trumpeter and composer Miles Davis should be regarded as an important constituent part of most of the trends over the last forty years. From the days of be-bop, when he played with Charlie Parker, to the current wave of rock/jazz, his name has remained at the forefront of the music. His 'Nonet', recorded in 1949 and 1950, blazed a trail for much of the 'cool school' material that followed. Despite a relatively quiet period in the early fifties, the classic quintet featuring John Coltrane emerged in mid decade, and he also entered the studio in the company of a large aggregation under the direction of Gil Evans to produce a handful of records of enduring quality. The 1960s had him heading another illustrious quintet including Wayne Shorter and Herbie Hancock, both to find themselves fame and fortune in the 'crossover' market. In 1969 two albums were recorded that paved the way for much of the jazz/funk that exists today: *In a Silent Way* and *Bitches Brew* sold in vast numbers unheard-of for records in the jazz idiom, and almost immediately the name of Miles Davis became popularized in other than jazz circles. Many of his subsequent live performances were to be in front of fervent rock-orientated audiences.

Of recent years the trumpeter's health has been poor, but towards the end of the eighties we find him well established again on the concert and festival tour circuit, delighting followers the world over. Never one to be blessed with the best of techniques, he nonetheless remains the great interpreter of whatever material he chooses to play. A handful of notes from the Davis horn can often be more meaningful than half a dozen choruses from many another trumpeter.

Houston Person   b. Florence, South Carolina, USA, 10 November 1934

Houston Person may not be regarded as a major artist in the jazz field but anybody who has been lucky enough to experience the tenor-player in live or recorded situations will know of the four-square solidity and uncompromising swing available on his menu.

His army service in Germany afforded him the luxury of time to play with Eddie Harris, Don Menza and Don Ellis. Upon returning home he toured for organist Johnny Hammond and eventually formed a band for himself. In 1973 an on-and-off partnership with singer Etta Jones became permanent, and the pair have made a considerable impact in clubs and concerts. The 1984 Nice Festival was a particularly notable triumph.

Bulee (Slim) Gaillard   b. Detroit, Michigan, USA, 4 January 1916

Slim Gaillard is best known for the duo he formed in the late 1930s with bass-player Slam Stewart. This team of the singing guitarist and the hum-along bass-player had an enormous success in the shape of *Flat Foot Floogie* in particular and other bizarre-sounding song titles in general. The singer and multi-instrumentalist then led a trio throughout the latter part of the forties, working the next twenty years in jazz clubs as well as variety shows, and in 1970 he and Slam briefly reunited at the Monterey Jazz Festival. A scat singer of note, he also found time to develop a kind of esoteric hip language called 'vout', unintelligible to all but the suitably initiated.

Currently residing in London and proving a popular figure on the scene, wearing the slanted beret and a beaming smile, Gaillard made a brief appearance in the ill-fated *Absolute Beginners*, not the first of a number of film parts. Undoubtedly, his being involved in *Hellzapoppin*, the zany film comedy of 1941, could not have been more appropriate.

Leroy (Slam) Stewart   b. Englewood, New Jersey, USA, 21 September 1914,
d. 10 December 1987

Slam Stewart played briefly with Peanuts Holland before deciding to throw in his
lot with Slim Gaillard to form the *Slim and Slam* duo of popular renown, but his
abilities were of a superior nature to the obvious novelty elements present in the
duo. He became Art Tatum's bass-player, an association lasting till the pianist's
death, and in 1945 recorded with Charlie Parker and Dizzy Gillespie, a surprisingly
successful date considering the rest of the band came out of the swing era.

The momentum carried on: in the *Benny Goodman Band*, leading a trio with
pianist Errol Garner, playing for Roy Eldridge and Clark Terry. In 1979 he
performed at the inaugural Capital Festival on the slopes in front of London's
Alexandra Palace. Festivals quite often attracted his attention! In 1987 an album
issued of a recording made half a dozen years earlier amusingly couples him with
another singalong bassist, Major Holley.

Albert J. (Budd) Johnson   b. Dallas, Texas, USA, 14 December 1910,
d. 20 October 1984

The history of Budd Johnson is a remarkable record of a musician who crossed over comfortably from one era to the next, coping with stylistic changes as they arose and gliding effortlessly through the ranks of countless bands. He claimed to have taught Ben Webster when they met up in Texas in 1928 but he definitely recorded with Louis Armstrong in 1933. Twelve months later he joined Earl Hines in a dual role of saxophonist and arranger, a part he was to play for the next eight years.

Be-bop held no qualms for him, and Dizzy Gillespie acted as his guide in the field. He recorded with everybody from Billy Eckstine and Pete Johnson to Joe Turner and Gil Evans – Evans' *Out of the Cool* features Budd. He toured the Soviet Union and South America in a small Earl Hines unit and left the pianist once again to form *JPJ* with Oliver Jackson, Bill Pemberton and Dill Jones, an extremely popular quartet.

His final recordings with Hines were made in 1977, and the last London sighting of him came in 1983, playing a foil to Jay McShann. With his death in 1984 jazz lost not only a fine saxophonist but a walking encyclopaedia covering all the important areas.

Albert Mangelsdorff   b. Frankfurt-am-Main, Germany, 5 September 1928

Trombonist Albert Mangelsdorff has the honour of being one of the very first Europeans to receive widespread recognition in the United States, figuring strongly in successive Down Beat polls. His standing is such that he is known to have influenced many of the young turks on the US side of the Atlantic, including George Lewis.

A bop-inspired musician, Mangelsdorff sought to establish an extension to the vocabulary of an instrument heavily dependent on the high-level proficiency of J.J. Johnson. He achieved his goal, surpassing the Johnson superlatives and establishing the Mangelsdorff style, a remarkable speciality being his utilization of multiphonics – meaning the ability to play chords. The Newport Festival in the sixties certainly helped perpetuate the trombonist's standing, as did the Jazz Expo 1970 concert in London, where he led his regular quartet of Heinz Sauer (tenor), Gunter Lenz (bass) and Ralf Hubner (drums). His teaming-up with French saxophonist Michel Portal lasted some considerable time, and he undertook a European tour with a trio completed by Wolfgang Dauner, Eddie Gomez and Elvin Jones.

The United Jazz and Rock Ensemble and a trio with Leon Francioli and Pierre Favre were two favourite slot holes for the eighties. A treat for British admirers materialized when, in 1986, London's Shaw Theatre was the venue for Mangelsdorff to meet John Surman, Dave Holland and Elvin Jones in a summit conference where all the powers agreed at the close of negotiations.

Alfred Antonius Josef (Ali) Haurand   b. Viersen, Germany, 15 November 1943

Ali Haurand had been seen with tenor titans Don Byas and Ben Webster before forming *Third Eye* in 1970, a group that would include Kenny Wheeler and Gerd Dudek amongst its members and with a lifespan running fifteen years. Almost simultaneously he joined the *European Jazz Quintet* and *SOH*, completed by Alan Skidmore and Tony Oxley. When *SOH* played the Camden Festival of 1983, Haurand applied a vibrator to the strings of his bass which amused the audience no end.

Despite respect from other musicians, Haurand is not very well known outside Western Europe, a situation that deserves to be rectified. The words of Barry McRae, reviewing the *Tony Oxley Quintet* at the 1985 Camden Festival, sum up his credentials: 'good gun-running pizzicato bass and sound arco work'. Nothing more need be said!

Lol Coxhill with Bruce Turner

Lowen (Lol) Coxhill   b. Portsmouth, Hampshire, UK, 19 September 1932

Lol Coxhill, saxophonist, actor, compère, singer and one-time busker, is one of the larger-than-life characters of the British jazz scene. Whether he is in the company of free improvisers like Evan Parker and Derek Bailey, playing as a soloist, fronting the *Recedents* or directing one of the many incarnations of the *Johnny Rondo Combo*, his calm and innate talent serves him well. Give him a standard to deal with and the most personal of statements will be forthcoming, tenor or soprano carrying equal weight and possibly abetted by the Coxhill vocal chords. His singing should be regarded as tongue-in-cheek but viewed from the aspect of his standing as a multi-faceted individual. The voice has been captured on record, but the instrumental contributions to *Company* albums, sparring with Steve Lacy and Anthony Braxton, his meeting Bruce Turner as the horn section for *Fingers Remember Mingus* and many personal efforts are what the real Lol is about.

However, who could possibly better him as MC for the annual Bracknell Festival? Under great pressure and not inconsiderable barracking from the audience, he holds the thing together with a mixture of charm, wit, one-line put-downs and, during lulls in the programme, an offering delivered from his soprano. It is not unknown for him to be infinitely more entertaining and musically accomplished than a number of the imported guests.

Adelaide Hall   b. Brooklyn, New York, USA, b. 1904-1909

Adelaide Hall toured in many a black revue before making her way to Britain and settling there in 1938. She had made her mark in the jazz world at a very much earlier date, when, in 1927, Duke Ellington used her wordless vocal to create a most evocative atmosphere in *Creole Love Call*, which she performed again at Duke's memorial service in 1974 at St Martin-in-the-Fields.

For the most part she continues to tour the world, as she has for over fifty years, and if the voice might not quite have the authority or quality of yesteryear, sheer professionalism gets her by.

One of the most delightful episodes of her life in recent years took place at a sparsely attended concert at London's Royal Festival Hall that presented singer Pearl Bailey. Pearl acknowledged Adelaide's presence in the audience, and Ms Hall responded in the only possible way – taking the microphone and delivering a joyfully swinging version of *I Can't Give You Anything But Love.*

Peter John King   b. Kingston-upon-Thames, Surrey, UK, 11 August 1940

Peter King is very near to being the British equivalent of Joe Henderson. His outstanding alto saxophone is universally acclaimed, the be-bop inspiration personally diluted to encompass later styles, permitting him entry into differing musical formations but somehow being taken for granted. At the opening of Ronnie Scott's first club in 1959, King embarked on a work schedule taking in the big bands of Johnny Dankworth, Maynard Ferguson, Tubby Hayes and Stan Tracey, pairing up with visiting Americans, a Ray Charles tour and backing singers Jimmy Witherspoon and Anita O'Day.

The *Be-bop Preservation Society* constituted a labour of love, the abandon of *Splinters*, the group co-led by drummers Phil Seaman and John Stevens, a chance to stretch out on less familiar ground, as was *Freebop* with its refusal to be classified. Only in the eighties did King lead a group anything like his own: supported by Henry Lowther, Dave Green and Spike Wells, he recorded for the Spotlite label. Stan Tracey continued to regard him as a regular component of both his octet and big band in the opening months of 1988.

Edward (Sonny) Stitt   b. Boston, Massachusetts, USA, 2 February 1924, d. 22 or 23 July 1982

The cross that Sonny Stitt had to bear for a good part of his life was the uncanny resemblance his playing bore to Charlie Parker's. Critics accused him of plagiarism, despite constant assurances that he had developed independently of the legendary alto saxophonist. The tone and phrasing certainly owed a debt to Parker, but slowly Stitt formulated a personal style that he extended to tenor and baritone. On top form he could be as exciting a performer as most saxophonists from his era.

Stitt arrived in New York after a short spell touring with the *Tiny Bradshaw Band* and slotted briefly into Billy Eckstine's big band, followed quickly by a transition to Dizzy Gillespie's group. Drug problems overtook him in the late forties but in 1950 he was back leading a band with tenorist Gene Ammons. The fifties included *Jazz at the Philharmonic* tours, a UK trip with Gillespie, Coleman Hawkins and Roy Eldridge and a short stopover with Gillespie again. He worked only in the best company: the sixties opened up opportunities to work in Miles Davis' band, to appear at a Newport Festival for a Parker tribute, to tour Japan in a sextet that included Clark Terry and to make his only visit to the Ronnie Scott club.

The *Giants of Jazz* package, which travelled widely in the early seventies, with Gillespie, Monk and Blakey, elicited some of Stitt's most adventurous blowing for some time – he was obviously relishing the close proximity of superior players.

Stitt died of cancer in 1982 but not before completing one of his happiest partnerships, with tenor-player Red Holloway.

Thomas (Tommy) Whittle   b. Grangemouth, UK, 13 October 1926

Tommy Whittle has long stood as a most respected tenor-player out of the mainstream/modern school who consistently proves his worth in all manner of musical areas. His days with Johnny Claes, Lew Stone and Harry Hayes, who also employed George Shearing, were a preliminary to his joining the popular Ted Heath band at the age of twenty, but boredom soon set in, the regimented atmosphere proving too much for a musician wishing to show his paces as a soloist. Finally he left to pass through Tony Kinsey's band and co-lead a quintet with baritonist Harry Klein that included the late pianist Dill Jones. Regular studio work in the ATV orchestra under the direction of Jack Parnell gave Whittle a steady income but he still liked to make appearances in clubs, sometimes in the company of his wife, singer Barbara Jay. For a while he ran a one-night-a-week jazz club at the Hopbine pub in Wembley that proved highly popular, and periodically he presented American artists such as Bud Freeman. He recently crossed swords on record with that fine reed-player Alan Barnes, allowing not an inch to a man half his age and giving the polished performance we have come to expect. A guest spot on a 1987 album under Helen Shapiro's name, *The Quality of Mercer*, received dutiful praise as well.

Humphrey Lyttelton   b. Windsor, Berkshire, UK, 23 May 1921

The playing career of the Old Etonian started with *George Webb's Dixielanders* but in 1948 he formed his own band, employing Webb, Wally Fawkes and the Christie brothers, Keith and Ian. A revivalist figure, he became extremely popular during the trad boom of the fifties, and in 1956 his 'Bad Penny Blues' made the top twenty records. Stylistically influenced initially by Louis Armstrong, he later became more commonly regarded as a devotee of Buck Clayton, with whom he was to work and record. Coming out of the decade, the band's style had changed, taking on a mainstream sound, due mainly to the addition of alto-player Bruce Turner, regarded as too modern by a number of the trumpeter's followers. This did not deter Humph from following his chosen path, and he has trodden the ground midway between the two styles, with varying degrees of success, ever since. Other skills were acquired along the way, and there are now a number of books published under the Lyttelton name. His weekly jazz programme for the BBC shows no signs of flagging, the vast knowledge of the presenter making it compulsive listening.

However, the playing side of life still looms large, and he can be frequently heard fronting the band, never afraid to change personnel when things appear to be getting stale. It would be difficult to envisage the British jazz scene without Humph's presence looming large.

69

Frederick Dewayne (Freddie) Hubbard   b. Indianapolis, Indiana, USA,
7 April 1938

In 1987 a disparate bunch of musicians toured Europe under the collective title of
Satchmo Revisited; amongst the personnel of this group (which was decidedly less
than artistically successful) was Freddie Hubbard. It was a strange situation, for a
musician whose impact came from entirely positive associations, working with Art
Blakey and Sonny Rollins and being tossed into the Ornette Coleman double
quartet recording *Free Jazz*. Other outstanding sessions to follow included *Blues
and the Abstract Truth, Ascension, Out to Lunch* and *Maiden Voyage*, all dates led
significantly by other musicians – Oliver Nelson, John Coltrane, Eric Dolphy and
Herbie Hancock respectively. Perhaps it was these important recordings that
initiated the belief, widely held, that Hubbard reserved his better playing for
performances away from his own bands. Trumpeter Ian Carr is the latest to
support this theory, in *Jazz, The Essential Companion*.

The seventies were not a creative period for Freddie Hubbard, despite the
album *First Light* winning a Grammy award. He had got bogged down in the
rock/jazz mire, and his normally assertive trumpet-playing lacked impact, although
he seemed quite happy with life when interviewed at Ronnie Scott's and meeting
Herbie Hancock & Co in *VSOP*, the Miles Davis quintet of the sixties, Hubbard
deputizing for Davis.

The eighties saw a turn back to a straight-ahead jazz policy, and the 1983
Camden Festival presented Hubbard's quintet with Hilton Ruiz and Herbie Lewis
as one of the main attractions. Freddie was back and blowing with fierce
determination.

Wayne Shorter   b. Newark, New Jersey, USA, 25 August 1933

Wayne Shorter joined Art Blakey in 1959, having worked with Maynard Ferguson and Horace Silver. At this juncture he was still struggling to rid himself of a style steeped in effects reminiscent of his major influence, John Coltrane, but by 1964, at the outset of his six years with Miles Davis, the sparer, melodic lines we recognize as a Shorter trademark had started to dominate. Davis found him a perfect front-line foil, and not only did Shorter contribute to the group as a musician but a number of his compositions shone out as band classics. *ESP, Nefertiti, Sanctuary* and *Paraphernalia* are attributable to him.

The seminal *In a Silent Way* and *Bitches Brew*, to which Shorter supplied the floating soprano saxophone, inspired him to leave Davis and form an electric band with Joe Zawinul, the resultant *Weather Report* influencing countless fusion outfits. The line-up of *Weather Report* changed intermittently but the two constant factors were Shorter and Zawinul. They continuously strived to retain a forward-looking policy, unlike some fusion bands, and if the majority of solos suffered from brevity, the compensation existed in fluctuating tone colours based on melodic extensions.

When *Weather Report* operations were suspended, well into the eighties, Shorter formed a band that vaguely inhabited similar territory but which lacked inspirational flair, his own playing suffering accordingly. Nevertheless, armies of young saxophonists have fallen under his spell, more likely because of his very special talents on soprano than from any ground-breaking work for the tenor he may have achieved.

73

Charles Edward (Charlie) Haden b. Shenandoah, Iowa, USA, 6 August 1937

It is difficult to believe that this outstanding bass-player commenced his career in New Orleans bands, for it was the innovative *Ornette Coleman Quartet* of the late fifties that helped forge the Haden reputation. In total accord with the great altoist's freedom message, he, more than any other, changed the traditional role of the bass-player to that of a major voice, particularly within the confines of the smaller ensemble. Never one to overplay the technical aspects of his craft, Haden emphasizes tone, drive and imagination.

Despite continued affiliation to things Colmanesque, one of his finest achievements to date must be leadership of the *Liberation Music Orchestra*, a group of musicians devoted to performance of Socialist-orientated works. Spanish Civil War and freedom movement songs rub shoulders in moving musical *montages* created by arrangers such as Carla Bley. However, the music stands up on its own merits, regardless of the listener's political leanings. Don Cherry, Dewey Redman and Mike Mantler are three musicians long associated with this important group.

His membership of the excellent *Keith Jarrett Quartet*, in the company of the aforementioned Redman and drummer Paul Motian, should also be regarded as a career highlight. In addition *Old and New Dreams*, a revival of the original Coleman band, minus the leader, proved to be an artistic success. Haden is in constant demand as a sideman in the bands of other leading modernists when he is not in the recording studio adding considerable talent to a number of marvellous sessions.

Donald E. (Don) Cherry　b. Oklahoma City, Oklahoma, USA,
18 November 1936

Trumpeter Cherry came to notice in the late fifties and early sixties, lending his inspired cornet improvisations to the *Ornette Coleman Quartet*. After brief working relationships with Steve Lacy and Sonny Rollins he became a founder member of the *New York Contemporary Five*. Adventurous partnerships involving Albert Ayler and Gato Barbieri helped to fuel his interest in music from other cultures, and a move to Sweden followed in the seventies.

Two projects took Cherry over in mid to late decade, the first being the formation of *Old and New Dreams* completed by Dewey Redman, Charlie Haden and Ed Blackwell, dedicated to a resurrection of the music and spiritual harmony of their days under Coleman's direction. The second involved a trio, utilizing the distinctive sounds of Colin Walcott, a sitar- and percussion-player, the remarkable Nana Vascencelos, also on percussion, plus Cherry himself, employing trumpet, flutes and a doussn'gouni, a very basic African guitar-like instrument.

His current band, *Nu*, includes Blackwell and Vascencelos and is completed by Carlos Ward (alto and flute) and Mark Helias (bass). This as yet unrecorded combination benefits from an open-minded attitude to the material it uses, engendering a fair amount of excitement and response from the paying customer.

Cherry is unquestionably a major figure from the last thirty years of development, his playing suitably laid down on vinyl, from nearly all the important peaks of creativity. The unabashed freedom employed in most of his chosen settings has never precluded a judicious use of space, the phrasing carefully unravelled, the note placement of supreme importance but always swinging mightily.

The World Saxophone Quartet, formed 1977

The WSQ consists of Hamiet Bluiett, Julius Hemphill, Oliver Lake and David Murray, four premier saxophonists who came together in the mid 1970s to perform a mixture of written and improvised works, most of which are penned by Hemphill. A mixture of reed instruments are employed to give the benefit of light and shade, in what can become a very predictable format – but not an accusation to be levelled at the WSQ.

A set delivered by the quartet pays homage to heritage in addition to the need for exploration, and each member in turn is allotted space to solo at length. Duos and trios formulate to give extra variety. Not the only saxophone quartet in existence, but certainly one that serves its purpose as a role model.

One or two substitutions in personnel had to be made recently, John Stubblefield and Branford Marsalis deputizing, but the original line-up appear on all the excellent records to date. The tribute to Duke Ellington from 1986 is as good an example of the WSQ at work as you could wish to find.

Hamiet Bluiett   b. Lovejoy, Illinois, USA, 16 September 1940

The St Louis orchestra of George Hudson (with its old-boy list including Clark Terry, Ahmed Jamal and Oliver Nelson) was where Bluiett gained invaluable experience, but exposure in the St Louis Black Artists Group in the late sixties helped him formulate musical ideas. A move to the Big Apple in 1969 found him caught up in the 'new music' of the Loft scene, balanced by the less tempestuous demands of work in the *Thad Jones-Mel Lewis Big Band*. He did lead a large unit for a while until problems set in and the idea died a death. In 1977 the *World Saxophone Quartet* came to fruition, and Bluiett took his place as the underpinning agent for fellow-saxophonists David Murray, Julius Hemphill and Oliver Lake.

Apart from the baritone, Bluiett also plays clarinet, and an ongoing passion is the *Hamiet Bluiett Clarinet Family*, the title suggesting the proliferation of clarinets in a constantly fluctuating personnel.

However, the large member of the reed family is his number-one instrument, and there is no better place to catch Bluiett than on *Birthright (A solo blues concert)* where vigorous ideas meet historical references head on to lay bare the musician's inimitable position in the 1980s. The track entitled *In Tribute To Harry Carney*, a free-ranging workout alluding to the instrument's first great exponent, tells us all we need to know about Hamiet Bluiett's sense of history.

Julius Hemphill   b. Fort Worth, Texas, USA, 1940

Julius Hemphill's breakthrough came when he moved to St Louis in 1968 and became a member of the Black Artists Group. He proceeded to forming a band including pianist John Hicks and worked with Anthony Braxton in Chicago and Europe. The seventies were to be a period of natural development, 'balanced contrast' best describing his movements between *Kool and The Gang, The World Saxophone Quartet* and self-perpetuating encounters. The proliferation of Hemphill compositions can be heard on his own *Coon Bidness*, the solo audio drama entitled *Roi Boye and the Gotham Minstrels* and the 1978 duo album with cellist Abdul Wadud, *Live in New York*. The cello/alto axis creates a beautifully balanced scenario, Hemphill veering between abstract lyricism and forthright exaltations.

The WSQ continues to draw on much writing and performing energy but Hemphill's JAH band unwinds spasmodically to perform music falling into the 'funk' category. He retains a constant need to extend himself beyond his already considerable achievements, harbouring an interest in poetry and multi-media events.

Oliver Lake   b. Marianna, Arkansas, USA, 14 September 1942

Possibly Oliver Lake is the true founder of the Black Artists Group, as the organization grew initially from his band. The 1973 Paris trip for the group presaged his move to New York and immersion in the lively 'loft' movement.

The records depicting his playing in that period indicate a shrugging-off of the Jackie McLean influence. *Heavy Spirits* traces a probing compositional route, the alto set in quintet, trio and solo formats, with three tracks incorporating a three-man violin section. The Toronto concert duets with trombonist Joseph Bowie disclosed the imaginative turn Lake had made. The WSQ enfolded his talents; he worked separately with Julius Hemphill, Leo Smith and others, forming *Jump Up*, a reggae band to add colourful contrast to his working life. The 1984 recording *Expandable Language* shows the potency Lake carries in his armoury of alto, soprano and flute, backed sympathetically by trombonist Kevin Eubanks, Geri Allen, Fred Hopkins and Pheeroan akLaff. All the WSQ albums are worthy of attention for his inventive and logical solos.

David Murray   b. Berkeley, California, USA, 19 February 1955

It is remarkable that only ten years have passed since the July evening at the Bracknell Jazz Festival when David Murray clambered onto a British stage for the first time and captivated a vociferous and excited audience. Stalking the stage *à la* Rollins, the tenor poured forth notes in a brazen display of virtuosity and with a keen awareness of the instrument's position in jazz history. If that wasn't enough, he returned to the UK a month later, heading a quintet, recorded live at London's Collegiate Theatre and confirmed what a significant composer/instrumentalist he already was at the age of twenty-three.

Coming from a background in the Church and R'n'B bands, Murray had become a familiar face on the New York 'loft' circuit, leading his own trios, sometimes with Mark Dresser and Stanley Crouch, often with Fred Hopkins and Phillip Wilson. He went on to work with James Blood Ulmer and *Jack DeJohnette's Special Edition* and in 1977 co-founded the *World Saxophone Quartet*. In the eighties he has alternated between fronting a quartet, represented by a beautiful album from 1979, *Morning Song*, an octet and a big band, both the latter superbly recorded on Black Saint in the studio, in addition to live performances from Sweet Basil's in New York. The personnel includes noted modernists, trumpeter Olu Daru, trombonist Craig Harris, saxophonists Steve Coleman, John Purcell, tuba-player Bob Stewart and drummer Billy Higgins. All the compositions and arrangements come from Murray himself. There is an immediacy and vitality about the whole concept of the larger units, a looseness in the ensemble anticipating the open-ended solos to follow.

Murray is comfortable performing inside and outside the given guidelines or structure of the most simple or demanding piece, regardless of tempo, his ballad-playing equal to his passionate outbursts on more fiery material. Compared initially with Albert Ayler, nobody now doubts that what we hear today is pure David Murray.

Brian Lemon   b. Nottingham, UK, 11 February 1937

Pianist Lemon arrived in London in the middle fifties and became part of the Freddy Randall band. Very quickly earning the respect of other musicians, jobs were to come his way from Dave Shepherd, George Chisholm and Danny Moss.

Seemingly confident in a number of varied settings, he often received invitations to back visiting Americans, and continues to carry out that function to the present day, particularly at London's Pizza Express. Since he had played with Benny Goodman, it appeared to be totally fitting that Bob Wilber should draft him into the 1987 re-creation that set out to reproduce the famous Big Band Carnegie Hall concert of 1938.

He is an accomplished pianist, never prone to excess, always ready to supply the fuel for others but invariably satisfying as a soloist. Perhaps it is indicative of his character that, on a 1970 record release entitled *Our Kind of Music*, he sat out on a couple of tracks despite the date being under his own name.

Harry (Sweets) Edison   b. Columbus, Ohio, USA, 10 October 1915

Alphonso Trents' band, *Eddie Johnson's Crackerjacks* and the *Jeter-Pillars* band were just three of Harry Edison's staging-posts leading to his thirteen-year conscription into the *Count Basie Band*, lasting from 1938 until 1950. Like many other ex-big band sidemen, he gravitated into the studios, playing for singers, including Frank Sinatra – he can be heard on many of the best Sinatra sides from the fifties. This was also a good era for Edison's own recordings: *Blues For Basie* in 1957 is one of the very best mainstream records including fine muted trumpet harnessed to unbeatable tenor and piano, supplied by Ben Webster and Oscar Peterson.

Singer Joe Williams left Basie at the beginning of 1961, and Edison formed a quintet to back him at the outset of a solo career. This lasted for a couple of years, but for the trumpeter the studios loomed large in his life in the sixties. *Edison Lights*, an album cut in 1976 for Pablo, indicated that Edison still contained some fire-power, always a requirement when tussling with Eddie 'Lockjaw' Davis and Count Basie. A recent offering, *Meeting In Stockholm*, with pianist Claes Crora, confirmed a continuing story of good musical health. Whilst never regarded as an over-inventive trumpeter, Sweets Edison carries a flame for the dependable individuals who constantly turn up the right phrase, eschew the vulgar option and brighten the dullest of gigs.

Courtney Pine b. Paddington, London, UK, 18 March 1964

Perhaps more words have been written in praise of the young Courtney Pine during the last half dozen years than many a jazz musician could expect in a lifetime. While much of the coverage can be viewed only as media hype, the serious music press has for the most part managed to retain a certain degree of balanced restraint in evaluating the talented newcomer.

Originally immersed in the funk and reggae mélange, he sought a more stimulating atmosphere for the bursting ideas he wished to develop and subsequently became involved in workshops run by drummer John Stevens. Soon the word was out that a virtually novice saxophonist had absorbed the language of Coltrane and clearly meant to spread the gospel amongst the traditionally non-jazz-listening black community.

Leading from the front, Pine gathered together a number of younger generation musicians prepared to devote themselves to the demands of improvised music. At the helm of a quartet, functioning as a mainstay of the all-black big band the *Jazz Warriors* or accepting various gigs under the direction of others, the Pine name is always in the limelight.

In 1986 he deputized for Sonny Fortune in the great Elvin Jones band to much acclaim, toured the UK with George Russell and at the Camden Festival took the stage with *Art Blakey's Jazz Messengers*. The Bath Festival of 1987 featured him as guest soloist with the *Orchéstre National* de Jazz.

His first record, *Journey to the Urge Within*, sold something like 70,000 copies, and Island Records are looking for a repeat from *Destiny's Song (& The Image of Pursuance)*. He may also be heard on the soundtrack of the film *Angel Heart*.

There is no argument that Courtney Pine stands as a gifted player, acquiring technical facility on tenor, soprano and bass clarinet, gradually cultivating the personal touch that should see him march boldly into the nineties.

84

**Branford
Marsalis**
b. New Orleans,
Louisiana, USA,
26 August 1960

The eldest of the brothers Marsalis has not been one to linger in the shadow of his much-publicized trumpet-playing brother Wynton, having already carved his niche very deeply into various musical frameworks. His father, the piano-playing Ellis, determined that all his offspring would benefit from a formal music education, and the young Branford received tuition on piano, then clarinet. This education continued in earnest when he became a conscript into the hotbed that is Art Blakey's band.

Leaving Blakey, he branched out in the company of Wynton, touring and recording with his band between 1982 and 1985 and also fitting in a Herbie Hancock tour. Eyebrows were raised when he, Kenny Kirkland, Darryl Jones and Omar Hakim were seconded by *Sting* for a globe-trotting series of concerts, but Branford clearly has an affinity with the rock star's music. The results of the collaboration were evident in the multi-million-selling *The Dream of the Blue Turtles*.

The contrasting melodies of *Romances for Saxophone* released in 1986 did not find eventual favour, Branford making some very uncomplimentary comments about the finished article, but other records under his belt must be viewed in a more positive light. *Think of One, Black Bones* and *Hot House Flowers* found him supporting Wynton admirably, but *Scenes in the City* and *Renaissance* are Branford projects, the latter showing him a fast-maturing exponent of the tenor and soprano saxophone. He cites Wayne Shorter as a major influence but recent indications promise a singularly personal approach on the horizon.

Clementina Dinah Campbell (Cleo) Laine   b. Southall, Middlesex, UK, 27 October 1927

Cleo Laine is a truly gifted singer, blessed with a remarkable range, a fluent technique and an enquiring musical brain. *The Johnny Dankworth Seven* and *Dankworth Big Band* of the early fifties were where she cut her teeth, and in 1958 she married Dankworth. Strangely enough, this was a signal for her to branch out into non-jazz fields, and Cleo has spread her net wide ever since. Film and stage parts came her way, including *The Roman Spring of Mrs Stone* in 1961. She performed in many differing contexts, with symphony orchestras and jazz groups, often as a double act with Dankworth and in shows like *Showboat*. She has an equally adoring public in the USA built up since her first visits in the seventies.

It is not necessary to categorize Cleo Laine: her repertoire stretches way beyond jazz, encompassing folk songs, popular songs, specially written compositions and light classical works. A singer *par excellence*.

Earl (Chico) Freeman Jnr.   b. Chicago, Illinois, USA, 17 July 1949

If ever a person was destined to become a musician, it's Chico Freeman. Coming from a musical family, father Von being the best known of the clan, Chico had a pre-planned destiny from the time he was born. Von Freeman's reluctance to move outside his native Chicago did not rub off on his son, and in 1976 Chico was working in New York. Don Pullen, Sam Rivers and Sun Ra, with whom his father had also worked, were soon to be part of an impressive list of employers. He came to Europe with Pullen and drummer Elvin Jones on separate occasions and returned once more for the 1982 Capital Jazz Festival at Knebworth.

He is now a familiar figure in the UK: Ronnie Scott's has played host to his quartet, the *Leaders* have visited twice, and in February 1988 Von and Chico played to packed houses at Scott's, neither man taking any prisoners in their two tenor clashes.

The younger Freeman, like most of his generation, was influenced by John Coltrane, but he has shown clear determination to construct a style independent of the great man without a slavish reliance on the current fads or fashions. That Chico is first and foremost a purist is borne out on such record releases as *Spirit Sensitive, Tangents, The Pied Piper* and the Leaders' *Mudfoot*. He exudes confidence on all three of his instruments, tenor, flute and bass clarinet, deserving the plaudits of the critics.

Grachan Moncur III   b. New York City, USA, 1937

As his father had been the bass-player with the original *Savoy Sultans*, Grachan Moncur was no stranger to the jazz life when in turn he took to the road with *The Jackie Wilson Show, Reggie Willis's Band* and Ray Charles. Art Farmer and Benny Golson's *Jazztet* constituted his musical home before New York residence brought him into the world of Sonny Rollins and Jackie Mclean.

Mclean added considerable authority to *Evolution*, considered Moncur's best recorded work. Archie Shepp employed him between 1967 and 1969, and the two-trombone team of Moncur and Rudd flaired convincingly on *Mama Too Tight*. The French BYG label released an album under his own name, and the *Jazz Composers Orchestra* featured one of his works.

He almost disappeared entirely from the international stage during the seventies, working the Newark area with organist Big John Patton. The eighties dawned with the Patton tie-in still going strong, and the decade saw Moncur appointed composer in residence at the Newark Community School of the Arts. Sweet Basil's in New York played host to the Archie Shepp band in 1987, Moncur flying once again for his old boss, and London merited a brief hearing from the trombonist, travelling with the *Paris Reunion Band*.

If the experimentation of the sixties tended to evolve directly from the tenor saxophonists, their alto counterparts, trumpeters and pianists, Moncur and Roswell Rudd were the two players ensuring a say on behalf of the beleaguered trombone.

Theodore Walter (Sonny) Rollins   b. New York City, USA, 7 September 1929

One of the true tenor giants, Rollins first made a reputation for himself as a member of the Max Roach/Clifford Brown group in the mid 1950s. He soon recorded the brilliant album *Saxophone Colossus* under his own name; it included the definitive version of the ever-popular calypso 'St Thomas'. Superior albums were to follow, such as the classic *Way Out West* and *The Freedom Suite*, a political statement which also showed Rollins' penchant for performing with only bass and drums, on this occasion in the company of Oscar Pettiford and Max Roach. Personal appearances turned into real *tours de force* until, unexpectedly, in 1959 the tenor player decided to retire for two years. He reappeared in the sixties, his style had not changed markedly but in 1967 retirement beckoned again for a period of five years.

A great individualist and commanding a passionate following, Rollins' assets are phenomenal. Even the flimsiest of melodies can gain unforeseen credentials when the fertile mind takes hold. The huge tone he employs can be distorted at the drop of a hat, harmonic conventions are thrown out of the window, rhythmic emphasis constantly being realigned. Even when operating at a lower level of creativity, his work exudes authority, and those wriggling codas that he unravels, particularly in ballads, are an aural treat.

Rollins' latterday performances have contained nods to the past but there does appear to be a preoccupation revolving around more lightweight material and a marked reluctance to stretch out in the company of musicians of equal status. Notwithstanding this state of affairs, Sonny Rollins still stands as the most influential of jazzmen.

Arthur Murray Blythe   b. Los Angeles, California, USA, 5 July 1940

Before making it to New York in 1974, alto saxophonist Blythe had worked in the band of pianist Horace Tapscott for ten years. He initially billed himself under the rather sinister title *Black Arthur*, but there certainly wasn't anything untoward about his credentials as a musician. Liaisons encompassing leading lights David Murray, Lester Bowie, Jack DeJohnette and the orchestra of Gil Evans allowed him to build a growing reputation.

Blythe is a most potent force on his chosen instrument, developing a style of its own, a kind of wailing lyricism, stemming from a background in the blues, and the pitching desperately fighting to stay in the right lane.

The best of Blythe is to be heard in the context of his group, featuring an unusual line-up that incorporates cello (Abdul Wadud) and tuba (Bob Stewart). The albums released by Columbia find a tight-fitting unit producing material of a lively, vibrant nature, creating a clearly stimulating atmosphere for the leader. *Elaborations* and *Light Blue* are excellent examples of consistent quality playing, although one or two of the recent records have a definite commercial bent.

Blythe can also be heard in the stellar confines of *The Leaders*, a sextet made up of heavyweight improvisers including Bowie, Chico Freeman and drummer Don Moye.

Kenneth (Kenny) Wheeler   b. Toronto, Canada, 14 January 1930

Kenny Wheeler arrived in Britain in the early fifties, playing in a succession of big bands and holding down a chair in *Johnny Dankworth's Band* from the late fifties to the mid sixties. The balanced view Kenny has always held stems from his preparedness to immerse himself in all aspects of the music, and the sixties opened his ears to possibilities inherent in the still developing work of John Stevens and Tony Oxley at outposts like the Little Theatre Club. Imagine the contrast of the *Mike Gibbs Orchestra* with the *Globe Unity Orchestra*, and the fearsome demands manifest in the *Anthony Braxton Quartet*, triggered by Dave Holland and Barry Altschul! The very different *Azimuth, United Jazz and Rock Ensemble* and *Dave Holland Quintet* tell of Wheeler's further need to vary his surroundings.

The ECM record label is the ideal place to go for Kenny Wheeler recordings with Keith Jarrett, Jan Garbarek and John Abercrombie or as the boss on a number of albums including the fine *Double, Double You*.

Samuel Carthorne (Sam) Rivers   b. El Reno, Oklahoma, USA, 25 September 1930

Reed-player Sam Rivers arrived in the Miles Davis group of 1964 via a working background tied in with singers, the *Herb Pomeroy Big Band* and countless other name players. He stayed the course for only a couple of months, finding the experience less demanding than he had hoped, and finally linked up with Cecil Taylor for five years and toured Europe, including an appearance at Jazz Expo 69, held at London's Hammersmith Odeon.

The stimulation of rubbing shoulders with the pianist and sidemen Andrew Cyrille and Jimmy Lyons broadened his outlook, and in 1971 Studio Rivbea, which he opened in conjunction with his wife, became one of the centres of the New York loft scene, then the main outlet for the more searching souls amongst the young improvisers.

Rivers then cultivated a lengthy and productive period with British bass-player Dave Holland, who seemed totally sympathetic to his ideas and aims. If visits to the UK are not as frequent as the British would like, such diverting moments as the evening he teamed up with Abdullah Ibrahim in an almost impromptu performance at the Camden Festival should be cherished.

Sam Rivers has always attempted a varied progression, encompassing solo concerts and working with a symphony orchestra. As saxophonist, flautist or composer, the highest standards have been sought and attained, the continuous search for the original rather than the commonplace evident in the extreme.

Abdullah Ibrahim (Adolph Johannes 'Dollar' Brand) b. Cape Town, South Africa, 9 October 1934

Pianist and composer Ibrahim played around Europe in the mid sixties, until Duke Ellington encouraged him to take the trip to the USA that would determine his future in the music world. Immediately becoming part of the *avant-garde* movement, he fell into the world of John Coltrane, Don Cherry and Ornette Coleman and recorded an outstanding album that found his talents matched by the equally passionate outpourings of Argentinian saxophonist Gato Barbieri. *Confluence* stands as one of his best records to this day.

Emerging onto the American scene, the influences of Monk and Ellington soon became apparent, allied to sounds from the townships, and an Ibrahim concert proved a unique experience whether solo or as part of a group.

Ibrahim has taken up many projects and pursued them restlessly, the latest band *Ekaya (Home)* being perhaps as creatively rewarding as anything tackled before. This septet, including Carlos Ward on alto and Ricky Ford's tenor, interprets the original compositions to perfection, the leader taking a back seat and letting the other musicians tell the story for him. Ward, a musician whose career appeared to be going nowhere, has emerged as a totally compatible soulmate, and he and the South African often branch out in tandem.

Politics inevitably lie very close to the surface of any Abdullah Ibrahim performance; often intensely felt vocals are included, and they should be regarded as an integral part of any concert.

His piano style still bows to the aforementioned masters, even more heavily percussive than of twenty years ago and building to painfully exciting climaxes. Melodic development runs a parallel course to produce a confection which the pianist serves up in the most compelling fashion.

99

Don Weller   b. Croydon, Surrey, UK, 19 December 1947

Weller first drew attention at the head of his jazz-rock band *Major Surgery* and in the various-sized units of Stan Tracey, the group he co-led with drummer Bryan Spring being one of the really exciting experiences of the last decade, the urgent and propulsive percusion work just the kind of springboard he prefers, his brand of uncomplicated, no-nonsense tenor rarely caught in a better situation. Visiting American trumpeters Ted Curson and Marvin Hannibal Peterson both reaped the benefits of the support they received from Spring/Weller & Co.

Gil Evans used Weller regularly for his UK tours of the eighties; Rocket 88 proved an occasional commitment, as did the mammoth Charlie Watts big band. For Don Weller on record, Weller/Spring's *Commit No Nuisance* serves him well as a front man, and two Tracey offerings, *The Bracknell Connection* and *The Salisbury Suite*, present a good picture of him as a sideman.

Kenneth Norville (Red) Norvo   b. Beardstown, Illinois, USA, 31 March 1908

The year 1925 had Norvo fronting a seven-piece marimba band, *The Collegians*, a stepping-stone to a stint in a Milwaukee ballroom and steady employment in the Victor Young NBC band. Paul Whiteman used him for a while, but he left taking Mildred Bailey (Mrs Norvo), the orchestra's singer, with him. Basing themselves in New York, they set up a couple of units of their own.

In 1943 the switch from xylophone to vibraphone occurred, and two years on he took a place in the Benny Goodman band – a short-lived stay that ended in a move to Woody Herman. Settling in California in 1947 didn't keep him away from New York, and he was soon back, first leading a trio that included Tony Scott, then a threesome with Charles Mingus and Tal Farlow.

Norvo continued the trio policy throughout the fifties but in 1959 he was in Europe touring with his old boss Goodman: thereafter he settled down in Las Vegas, working such venues as the Sands Hotel. Retiring briefly in 1972-3, he then took up the mallets once more, playing dates on both East and West Coasts and returning to Europe.

A highly influential practitioner, eschewing the more obvious percussion aspects of his instrument as demonstrated by the more showmanlike Hampton, Norvo concentrates on the more ethereal and subtle tones available to the discerning performer.

103

John Birks (Dizzy) Gillespie   b. Cheraw, South Carolina, USA, 21 October 1917

Alongside Charlie Parker, Dizzy Gillespie is regarded as the founder of be-bop and consequently the daddy of modern trumpet-playing. His ability to play at high speed in whatever register, combined with a fierce swinging attack and unlimited invention, singled him out as the yardstick by which other trumpeters were judged.

Dizzy learnt his trade in the big bands of the thirties, joining the *Teddy Hill Band* in 1937 to replace the great Roy Eldridge. Stays with Earl Hines and Cab Calloway, by whom he was sacked for clowning around, followed before a period playing and arranging for Billy Eckstine. In 1945 and 1946, years that were to become highly significant, he formed a playing and recording association with Parker. The classic tracks laid down in that period, such as *Groovin' High, Salt Peanuts, Shaw Nuff* and *Hot House* found both hornmen in inspired form. A big band assembled at the time employed exciting examples of the new music, in addition to Latin-American tunes, a *genre* that has always fascinated Dizzy. The 1950s were to find him leading another big band, this time for a US State Department tour. The sixties and seventies proved to be one long round of tours and recording, a newly acquired contract for Norman Granz' Pablo label seeming to lend to a new lease of life in the company of contemporaries like Count Basie and Oscar Peterson.

If he nowadays seems to rest on his well-merited laurels from time to time in live performance, there always exists the chance that a spark will suddenly ignite the old flame and sparks begin to fly. The man's contribution to the development of improvised music is enormous, his place in history assured.

James Moody   b. Savannah, Georgia, USA, 26 March 1925

James Moody often claims that his fame evolves from the 1949 King Pleasure recording of *Moody's Mood for Love*, which turned into a hit for the singer. Most people would point to the Dizzy Gillespie years and suggest that his own characteristic tenor, alto and flute-playing are the reasons for reverence.

The *Gillespie Big Band* had featured Moody as a soloist prior to his arrival in Paris in 1948, and one year later he was appearing at the Paris International Jazz Festival with the *Miles Davis/Tadd Dameron Quintet*. He went on to lead a septet back in the USA, carrying a lifespan of nine years, singers Babs Gonzales and Eddie Jefferson as members.

In 1963 he returned to the Gillespie quintet for five years, finally going out on his own, moving to Los Angeles and resigning himself to the obscurity of a sideman in Las Vegas club bands. Thankfully he threw off the cloak and re-emerged to perform widely, touring Europe and being seen at the Capital Festival with Gillespie in 1981. Neither is he a stranger to Ronnie Scott's.

As a saxophonist Moody is an eloquent, polished performer; as a flautist, he is arguably one of the foremost and most effective exponents, pure of tone, faultless in articulation.

Sheldon (Shelly) Manne   b. New York City, USA, 11 June 1920,
d. 26 September 1984

Manne dabbled for a short while with the saxophone before swapping the instrument for a set of drums, taking Jo Jones as his inspiration. Initially, the boats to Europe were a source of employment but, growing disenchanted at the music he was asked to play, he became land based in the bands of Will Bradley and Les Brown. Moving on to Stan Kenton, Woody Herman and the sextet of Charlie Ventura, he eventually made his way to the West Coast, becoming involved with Shorty Rogers. In 1954 he decided to become his own boss but in 1957 he did find time, along with Ray Brown, to add masterful touches to Sonny Rollins' magnificent *Way Out West* album.

Plenty of freelance employment and the opening of his club, Shelly's Manne Hole, in Los Angeles kept him busy in the sixties and into the seventies, when the LA4 burst onto the scene, the drummer joined by Ray Brown, Laurindo Almeida and Bud Shank. The lucrative field of composing for films and TV also opened up for him but did not preclude his continued appearances on the jazz merry-go-round. In 1979 Manne told the late distinguished Sinclair Traill: 'I am more interested in the art of drumming than the technique and have always tried to make the drums as much a musical instrument as possible.' When he died, in 1984, he had more than fulfilled that aim.

Salvatore (Sal) Nistico   b. Syracuse, New York, USA, 2 April 1940

Nistico emerged from the Mangione brothers' band of the early sixties to work for both Count Basie and Woody Herman. The Herman connection was to last for many years, and he cropped up in a number of editions of the band, leaving behind him a legacy encapsulated on such Herman LPs as *Encore, Woody's Winners, Light My Fire* and *World Class*. The forceful and fat-toned tenor is ideal for the section of a band with a reputation for its full-throttle exercises. The seventies brought a move to Europe, where Nistico had toured with Slide Hampton, and a 1976 recording, *Just For Fun*, accompanied by a German rhythm section, recaptures some of his best work from the sixties. The octet led by George Coleman, including Sal Nistico, Frank Strozier, Harold Mabern and Billy Higgins, made quite an impression at the beginning of this decade, Sal often matching his leader in creativity and power.

Stephen W. (Steve) Swallow   b. New York City, USA, 4 October 1940

Bassist and composer Steve Swallow already had that 'quality' label when he arrived in the Stan Getz quartet of 1965, a group brimming over with talent, for, apart from the leader, the virtuoso vibes-playing of Gary Burton and the stylish drumming of Roy Haynes were on offer. When Burton departed, Swallow went as well and joined forces with him for three years, until moving to San Francisco. A short return to the Burton fold preceded an association with Mike Gibbs of which recorded evidence exists in *The Only Chrome Waterfall Orchestra* and *In the Public Interest*.

The bass guitar, rather than the upright model, became Swallow's premier mode of expression during these years; when entering the world of Carla Bley in the late seventies, he used it almost exclusively. The Bley connection has lasted to the present, but Swallow certainly hasn't limited his horizons in the eighties, playing in the *John Scofield Trio*, associating with New York composer/arranger Kip Hanrahan and producing Scofield's last three successful albums. If initially Steve Swallow formed his reputation on the basis of being an excellent musician, it is true to say that playing has been pushed slightly into the background by his composing and arranging.

Billy Higgins   b. Los Angeles, California, USA, 11 October 1936

When Billy Higgins joined the *Ornette Coleman Quartet* in the late fifties, it was a case of the pupil beating the master to the punch. His mentor Ed Blackwell could not make the original line-up, so with both youthful hands, Higgins grasped the opportunity to embrace the radical teachings of Coleman. The drumming on *The Shape of Jazz to Come* indicates the sharpness and ability to learn quickly that encouraged so many of the music's predominant figures to hire him.

Adaptability brought him work with Sonny Rollins, John Coltrane, Thelonious Monk, Hank Mobley, Dexter Gordon and Jackie McLean. McLean's direction-changing *New And Old Gospel* sports Higgins laying down the rhythmic patterns for the altoist and Coleman on trumpet. Coleman would invite him back temporarily; Cedar Walton and Clifford Jordan claimed him as their regular drummer; George Coleman thrived with his octet and quartet driven by Higgins.

Guitarist Pat Metheny obviously knew a thing or two, choosing the drummer and Charlie Haden for his *Rejoicing* album, and the *David Murray Big Band* could not want for a better time-keeper. Wherever Billy Higgins performs, musicians and followers alike may rest assured the band will swing, due to the unobtrusive but permanently switched-on drummer. The easy flow generated from his floating hands certainly makes the percussion art look like a less arduous physical proposition than it actually is.

John Arnold (Johnny) Griffin III   b. Chicago, Illinois, USA, 24 April 1928

At seventeen years of age Johnny Griffin sat in the saxophone section of the Lionel Hampton band alongside Arnett Cobb, a rigorous apprenticeship lasting two years but an eminently suitable education for the man destined to find equally demanding employment with Art Blakey and Thelonious Monk in the fifties. Absorbing the spirit of Monk's philosophy, he acquired a reputation as having 'the fastest fingers in the West', able to deal with complicated chord changes and super-human tempos without breaking sweat – and, more importantly, saying something worthwhile on the journey.

He lived in Paris in the late sixties, playing and recording with the *Kenny Clarke-Francy Boland Band*, making three excellent albums in 1967 as he was caught in the act at Copenhagen's Montmartre Jazzhuis in sparkling form. He would sporadically get together with an old sparring-partner, Eddie 'Lockjaw' Davis, to recreate the joyful partnership first cemented in the States.

Now resident in the Netherlands, he still makes periodic visits to his home country but the lion's share of his performing takes place in his adopted Europe, often with touring Americans such as old friend Dexter Gordon or celebrating with ex-pats in the *Paris Reunion Band*.

Somebody once declared that Johnny Griffin was incapable of giving a bad performance, and that is difficult to argue against. His consistency over a period exceeding forty years has been a remarkable achievement.

Arthur Edward (Art) Pepper b. Gardena, California, USA, 1 September 1925, d. 15 June 1982

This West Coast saxophonist successfully trod the ground between the 'cool' approach and the more aggressive stance of New-York-influenced players. At the age of eighteen he worked in the *Benny Carter Orchestra*, followed by occasional stints with Stan Kenton until 1952. Dependency on drugs meant that he dropped out from the scene for varying intervals, and later years were to feature stays in gaol and in hospital for surgery and drying-out.

A series of albums in the late fifties for the Contemporary label contain Pepper's best recorded work, revealing a melodic side to his nature that carried a certain emotional edge reflective of mounting personal problems. The succeeding decade proved to be far from kind to the alto-player, and he was reduced to scuffling for work in rock bands. Subsequently the middle to late seventies found him touring Europe and Japan displaying a harder tone that gave him new-found authority.

This brief resurgence in Pepper's checkered career eventually had to give way to the ravages of his previous lifestyle, and he died in 1982.

Robert Coull (Bobby) Wellins   b. Glasgow, UK, 24 January 1936

Coming from a musical family, Wellins' playing experience was gained in the orchestras of Tony Crombie and Vic Lewis. A mutually rewarding association with Stan Tracey reached a pinnacle in 1965 when the pianist's *Under Milk Wood* suite was recorded and received much critical acclaim. However, this virtually heralded a near ten-year break for the saxophonist, due to insurmountable personal problems, but in 1976 Don Weller and he formed a quartet, proving inconclusively that Bobby Wellins was back with a bang.

Lol Coxhill figured as a partner in a free-flowing duo confrontation, and another quartet, propelled by drummer Spike Wells, started to receive regular work.

In the eighties the personal style he has achieved is impressive, a synthesis of many influences, delivered in seemingly effortless fashion. Sat in the saxophone section of the *Charlie Watts Orchestra* or battling a quality American like Teddy Edwards, as he did in one memorable night at London's 100 Club in 1987, true originality is the name of the game.

John Scofield   b. Ohio, USA, 26 December 1951

At a young age guitarist Scofield played in rock bands, a background that eventually opened the door to a place in Billy Cobham's fusion band of 1975. After two years he left to replace Pat Metheny in the Gary Burton group. In fact, 1977 turned out to be a significant year: recording his first album for the Enja label, making a studio date for Charles Mingus and taking a band out on the road under his own leadership for the first time.

Towards the end of 1982, Scofield got a call to join Miles Davis and, sharing a good percentage of solo duties with saxophonist Bob Berg as the trumpeter gave them more space, his blues-based offerings emerged as an important component in the band's overall concept. He also made telling contributions to the albums *Decoy* and *You're Under Arrest*.

Leaving Davis as a more commanding individual, he took to the road again, this time carrying a 'major artist' tag, now needing no verification after the release of three melodic and inventive records on the Gramavision label. *Electric Outlet, Still Warm* and *Blue Matter* are excellent examples of the ease and fluency he brings to guitar-playing, his very individual technique of delaying notes beyond the beat adding a special kind of tension.

In an interview published in *Wire* magazine (May 1986), Scofield told critic Brian Priestley: 'There was a time when I would play rock'n'roll licks on one thing and jazz licks on another. But I think, thank God, that that's come to an end and that I'm able to live in both worlds.' Apart from Pat Metheny, there are indeed few guitarists like 'Sco' who have a successful foot in both camps.

Sun Ra (Herman 'Sonny' Blount)   b. Birmingham, Alabama, USA, May 1910-15

A somewhat eccentric and exotic figure of indeterminate age, Sun Ra attracts audiences as much for the visual appeal of his Arkestra as for its music. It is remarkable to think that his distant associations, which include Coleman Hawkins and Fletcher Henderson amongst their number, should have led the band-leader along the path to the *avant garde*/new thing movement of the sixties.

His concerts and club dates have frequently incorporated wild, free-blowing passages in conjunction with fire-eaters and back-projected film, with dancers and musicians, sometimes in colourful costumes, joining the assembled throng in a 'walkabout'. Despite the hit-or-miss flavour of much of the experimentation, such fine players as John Gilmore, Pat Patrick, Marshall Allen and Alan Silva have stayed loyal to this mysterious figure for lengthy periods of their careers.

In the 1980s Ra is taking a backward look, introducing swing band arrangements, rhythm and blues and more accessible material into what has almost become a cabaret act, albeit of a stimulating nature. His somewhat shambolic attitude to live performance somehow typifies the spirit of jazz in an era loaded down by po-faced presentation. Ra claims to be an interglactic visitor to Earth, and if this could be regarded as remotely true, perhaps we should be cocking an ear heavenward to give ourselves a preview of the shape of jazz to come.

Danny Moss   b. Sussex, UK, 16 August 1927

Danny Moss is a descendant of the classic tenor teaching of Lester Young, Coleman Hawkins, Don Byas and Ben Webster. When in full flight, he will frequently allude to the syntax the great masters perfected, whilst dismissing any suggestion of mere plagiarism. His big band track record is first class, the Ted Heath and Johnny Dankworth bands high on the list of credits from the past, the present represented by the densely populated Charlie Watts juggernaut and the recent Benny Goodman re-creation under Bob Wilber's leadership.

Since the sixties Moss has also worked in the smaller groups of Alex Welsh, Humphrey Lyttelton and Freddy Randall. *The Pizza Express All Stars*, backing singer Tony Bennett, and the quartet he co-leads with Brian Lemon have also contributed to a busy schedule in the last handful of years.

Al Grey, Tony Scott and Buddy Tate

George Holmes (Buddy) Tate   b. Sherman, Texas, USA, 22 February 1915

Buddy Tate had resided in the bands of Terence Holder, Andy Kirk and Nat Towles before the historic move in 1939 to the *Count Basie Orchestra*, where of course one of his section mates was Lester Young. Nine years were to pass before he left the organization, finding employment with Lucky Millinder, Hot Lips Page and Jimmy Rushing.

Tate continued to find regular work, mixing recording dates, touring extensively and enjoying a residency at New York's Celebrity Club that lasted over twenty years. In 1972 he appeared at the Newport Jazz Festival in a special edition of the *Benny Carter Orchestra*, filled out by such illustrious names as Dicky Wells, Budd Johnson, Teddy Wilson and Jo Jones – a band that deserved to be recorded. In 1980 tenorist Jimmy Forrest died and Tate stepped into the breach, continuing the tenor/trombone twosome that Forrest had formed with Al Grey, a duo still alive and well in 1988.

Buddy Tate is clearly one of the few genuine remaining exponents of a lineage traced back to Coleman Hawkins. Many contemporary players may have greater technical facility but very few can swing harder than the man from Texas.

Albert Thornton (Al) Grey   b. Aldie, Virginia, USA, 6 June 1925

The wide grin, seemingly a permanent feature across the face of Al Grey, suitably represents his attitude to trombone-playing and to the music he selects to perform. The 'last of the greater plungers' tag, bestowed upon him as one of the remaining skilful users of the plunger mute, affords him a unique place among fellow trombonists. Minus the mute, his fat, brassy tone conjures up an irresistible urge to compare him with the great slide men of yesteryear, Kid Ory, Tricky Sam Nanton, Jack Teagarden and Bill Harris amongst them.

Devotees of the *Count Basie Band* affectionately remember his telling contribution to various editions of the band, but when first joining the Count in 1957, Al had previous experience with Lucky Millinder, Benny Carter, Jimmy Lunceford and Dizzy Gillespie to bring with him.

Inevitably the Basie connection looms large in any Grey biography, but his tours with *Jazz at the Philharmonic*, recordings wide ranging enough to include Quincy Jones and Louis Armstrong, the band he co-led with Billy Mitchell and the trombone/tenor package first with Jimmy Forrest, currently Buddy Tate in harness, should not be overlooked.

The good-time trombone of Al Grey receives a warm welcome at clubs, concerts and festivals on a global basis.

Tony Scott (Anthony Sciacca)   b. Morristown, New Jersey, USA, 17 June 1921

After leaving the Juilliard School in 1942, Tony Scott spent over twelve years splitting his time between employment with the likes of Buddy Rich, Earl Bostic, Claude Thornhill and Duke Ellington (a none-too-happy four weeks) and leading his own bands, at some time including Dizzy Gillespie plus Babs Gonzales. A tour to Europe in 1957 set him on the road to a lifetime of journeying in exotic parts, seeking out differing ethnic cultures and the music attributed to them. He spent the early sixties in the Far East, then returned to America and an almost inevitable coming-together with fellow ethnic-musicologist Colin Walcott, resulting in the record esoterically entitled *Music for Yoga Meditation and Other Joys*.

A permanent move to Italy prompted further journeyings in both Western and Eastern Europe, occasionally producing some eccentric and bizarre encounters – for instance, the 1977 meeting with *The Traditional Jazz Studio of Prague* produced a strangely off-centre album called *Boomerang*, featuring Scott on tenor and clarinet, the saxophone solos clearly at odds with the rest of the band.

However, the Czech experience is indicative of this maverick's philosophy, ever ready to immerse himself in multifarious musical situations, his clarinet work forever recognizable as undiluted Tony Scott.

Joseph Dwight (Joe) Newman b. New Orleans, Louisiana, USA, 7 September 1922

Joe Newman joined the *Lionel Hampton Big Band* in 1941 and a couple of years later gained his first footing in the Count Basie band. This was an on-and-off stay that lasted until 1947 when the trumpeter took a job with ex-Hampton tenor saxophonist Illinois Jacquet. A few years later he returned to the Basie fold and was featured trumpeter from 1952 to 1961. When he left for the second time, he led his own band but found his time being increasingly spent as a teacher and publicist for the music.

Nonetheless, Newman exists as a fine, commanding player of the mainstream persuasion who often doffs his cap in a more modern direction. He can still be heard in live sessions backed by local rhythm sections and as part of a traditionally swinging big band.

Malachi Favors b. Chicago, Illinois, USA, 22 August 1937 *or* Lexington, Mississippi, USA, 27 August 1937

Playing with pianist Andrew Hill, associations with Roscoe Mitchell's sextet, out of which the *Art Ensemble of Chicago* developed, and Richard Abram's *Experimental Band*, that fathered the AACM (Association for the Advancement of Creative Music), helped to bring Favors' name to the forefront of the music. His imagination and bold attacking style, influenced by Wilbur Ware, mark him down as an outstanding bass player. He has been a permanent fixture in the AEC since its formation in the late sixties. There is no back seat for Favors, as his large tone cuts through the ensemble or as he plays a full part in the frequent percussion interludes.

The AEC's vast library of recorded work, affords us numerous examples of Favors' invaluable contribution to one of the premier improvising bands.

Locksley Wellington 'Slide' Hampton   b. Jeannette, Pennsylvania, USA, 21 April 1932

The left-handed trombonist, composer and arranger 'Slide' Hampton is yet another American jazzman whose stay in Europe did nothing to harm a growing reputation. The former Maynard Ferguson sideman arrived in Britain in 1968 with Woody Herman, settled briefly in Berlin and eventually went to Paris for a six-year residency. He had originally spent formative years in the groups of Art Blakey, Dizzy Gillespie and Max Roach, the early sixties finding him bossing an octet including George Coleman, Freddie Hubbard, Booker Little and Julian Priester.

On returning to New York in 1977, he became involved in tuition and formed the *World of Trombones*, which grew into a twelve-piece band, featuring no fewer than nine trombonists. Visits to Europe are not infrequent, and in 1986 the *New York All Stars* undertook a tour, Slide well to the fore at the North Sea extravaganza and the Nice Jazz Festival.

A gifted musician, articulate and fluent in execution, he openly acknowledges a debt to the be-bop mastery of J.J. Johnson, upon whose style he constructed a free-flowing extension.

Lester Bowie and Richard Purcell Brown

Lester Bowie   b. Frederick, Maryland, USA, 11 October 1941

One of the original members of the AACM (Association for the Advancement of Creative Musicians) in Chicago, Bowie became the central figure of the *Art Ensemble of Chicago* formed in conjunction with Roscoe Mitchell in 1969. An inspired improvising ensemble including Joseph Jarman, Malachi Favors and Don Moye, the AEC conjure up an intoxicating brew of wild, free improvisation, compelling percussion passages and elements firmly established at the heart of jazz. Body-paint was used by members in the past to create atmosphere and a sense of theatre but, holding centre-stage, Bowie, resplendent in white doctor's coat, trumpet pointing skywards, would pinpoint the direction the music would next take.

Finding time to record in the company of Archie Shepp and Cecil Taylor sharpened his already unique style, a mixture of pure tone, jungle-like growls, almost inaudible whispering lines and punchy, authoritative statements. Despite continued involvement in the AEC, the trumpeter still sought further extensions to his career, and so he set up *From the Roots to the Source*, using ex-wife soul-singer Fontella Bass on vocals. This was in turn a mere stepping-stone to *Brass Fantasy*, comprising eight brass-players, Stanton Davis and Steve Turre amongst them, plus drummer Phillip Wilson, a long-time associate. *Fantasy* was made up of alternate straight-ahead jazz pieces and popular songs that took the leader's fancy. *Thriller* and *Personality* came off the last album; *Saving All My Love For You* and *Blueberry Hill* from the previous one – maybe all a little tongue-in-cheek but there is no doubting the collective effectiveness of the nonet in full cry.

If the numerous sides recorded under the auspices of the *Art Ensemble* indicate the trumpeter's improvisational prowess, the *Brass Fantasy* tracks and entertaining live concerts show the reverse side of the coin, where the obvious need to communicate with a slightly different public is paramount.

135

Edward B. (Ed) Blackwell b. New Orleans, Louisiana, USA, 1927 or 1929

Ed Blackwell first met Ornette Coleman in New Orleans in 1949, making a lasting impression that resulted in his making a journey to New York in 1960 to replace Billy Higgins in the altoist's now legendary quartet. There followed a decade of intense playing and recording with most of the leading lights of the period, his supreme percussion abilities finding favour with Don Cherry, Archie Shepp, Eric Dolphy and Randy Weston, in whose company he spent a year in Morocco. Records such as the famous double quartet date, organized by Coleman and entitled *Free Jazz, Where Is Brooklyn* and *Mu: (First & Second Parts)*, supporting trumpeter Cherry, clearly elevated the drummer into the upper echelons of the jazz hierarchy.

At the beginning of the seventies he rejoined Coleman and took up a teaching post at Wesleyan University, but for the past fifteen years he has required regular use of a kidney-machine, which tends to limit his availability for work. However, 1976 saw him taking up with ex-Coleman colleagues in *Old And New Dreams*, and more recent days find him bound up again with Cherry in the pleasing surroundings of the *Nu* group.

Blackwell is a unique drummer, who, despite a dedication to the now accepted group role the instrument has acquired, never forsakes his New Orleans roots, an aspect immediately apparent when he is fulfilling a pure time-keeping function.

David (Dave) Holland   b. Wolverhampton, UK, 1 October 1946

The manner in which Dave Holland found himself becoming a member of Miles Davis' band is now part of jazz folklore. Playing behind singer Elaine Delmar at Ronnie Scott's, he struck a chord with the legendary trumpeter who was sitting in the audience, and within a month he was in New York as Davis' bass player. For two years he stuck with the line-up that included Wayne Shorter and Chick Corea, recording on *Filles de Kilimanjaro, In a Silent Way* and *Bitches Brew* in the process. The band also appeared at London's Jazz Expo in 1969.

Holland and Corea left Davis to form *Circle*, a relatively short-lived but stimulating group that included Anthony Braxton and Barry Altschul. There then followed a period spent working variously with Betty Carter, Joe Henderson, Jack DeJohnette, Paul Bley and Sam Rivers. A permanent concentration on the Rivers union produced a mutual transference of ideas, committed to record on two New York albums from 1976.

His current band of Kenny Wheeler, Julian Priester, Steve Coleman and Marvin 'Smitty' Smith appears to satisfy the need to perform constantly with other restlessly searching individuals who are aware of the growing demand for group empathy.

Always a virtuoso bass-player, Holland has extended his role to composing and as head of jazz studies at the Banff School of Fine Arts in Alberta, Canada. One of Britain's finest exports!

Theodore (Ted) Curson   b. Philadelphia, Pennsylvania, USA, 3 June 1935

The highly regarded trumpeter Ted Curson formed a potent horn team partnering Eric Dolphy in the *Charles Mingus Quartet* during the years 1959 and 1960 – a short stay but long enough for him to appear on one of the bass-players' greatest records, *Charles Mingus Presents Charles Mingus*. The solos are brilliantly conceived and the interplay between alto, trumpet, bass and drums is glorious in execution.

In 1966 *Downbeat* magazine honoured Curson by awarding him the New Trumpet Star accolade in the annual critics poll, but by that time he lived in Europe. He continued to play clubs in both New York and Paris for a number of years, finding himself in Zurich in 1973 performing non-jazz works in the grandly named *Schauspielhaus Theatre Orchestra*.

Curiously enough, he did not work in the UK until the 1983 Bracknell Jazz Festival, making up for lost time by taking the stage in both the *Graham Collier Big Band* (a performance captured on film for Channel Four) and the *Don Weller/Bryan Spring* group. He still proves in the eighties to be a creative force to be reckoned with.

Bob Stewart   b. Sioux Falls, South Dakota, USA

The tuba is not an instrument readily associated with post-war movements in the jazz field, its role having long been usurped by the string bass and its image relegated to fossil status. However, the tuba was not permitted to die and, in the hands of the few, still maintained a minor place on the contemporary stage. Red Callender continued to use it occasionally; Ray Draper recorded with both John Coltrane and Max Roach in 1958; Howard Johnson held his own on the raucous Archie Shepp album *Mama Too Tight* and went on to lead a tuba ensemble which included one of his pupils, Bob Stewart.

Stewart brings a new dimension to tuba-playing, mirroring the fluency of many a trombonist or baritone saxophonist and consequently able to take a full part in group and solo duties. His credits include regular work with Arthur Blythe, Carla Bley, Gil Evans and *Lester Bowie's Brass Fantasy*, for which he supplies some decidedly funky bass figures. Charlie Haden had also used him in one of his versions of *The Liberation Music Orchestra*.

Band-leading has taken a back seat. For a while he co-led a quartet with French-horn-player John Clark, but presently the *First Line Band* with *Fantasy* colleagues Steve Turre and Stanton Davis in attendance is the direction he's taking. Whichever way he may turn in the future, his sterling efforts have totally dispelled the notion of the tuba's being a slave to its undistinguished history.

Harold (Hal) Singer   b. Tulsa, Oklahoma, USA, 8 October 1919

Singer built a reputation within the confines of such big bands as Lloyd Hunter's Serenaders (1939), Ernie Fields, Tommy Douglas (1941), Nat Towles (1942) and Jay McShann (1943), whom he joined not long after the departure of Charlie Parker. Having spent a few months in the Lucky Millinder band in 1948, he left for a brief stay with Duke Ellington, during which time he recorded *Cornbread*, a tune that proved to be a great hit, allowing him the chance to take a band of his own out on the road. For much of the following decade he earned a living playing in the rock 'n' roll field.

In 1965 Singer made a home in Europe, again popping up in big bands fronted by Johnny Dover and Slide Hampton but not neglecting his personal credentials as a bandleader. Appearances in Paris clubs were frequent, between many festival engagements and visits to the recording studios.

Perhaps not the most creative of tenor-players, Singer still represents that body of uncomplicated, big-toned, straight-down-the-road saxophonists carrying the flag for the traditions of the instrument.

Elvin Ray Jones   b. Pontiac, Michigan, USA, 9 September 1927

The youngest of three Jones brothers, Hank and Thad being the others, Elvin is justly fêted as one of the great drumming innovators. The years he spent as a member of the *John Coltrane Quartet* in the early sixties helped to turn round the thinking of a whole generation of percussionists. Coltrane's experimentation demanded a backdrop to give him space and freedom: in Elvin Jones, pianist McCoy Tyner and bassist Jimmy Garrison his prayers were answered. Elvin put down a polyrhythmic base of almost raw intensity, against which Coltrane was able to unravel complex solos, without the limitations imposed by normally signposted accents. Elvin's accents were extremely personal and could be delivered from any part of the kit.

After the Coltrane experience, any situation, would necessarily be an anti-climax, but the drummer formed his own trio with Joe Farrell and Garrison, the first of a series of small groups, satisfying in their own way but inevitably lacking the intensity of the Coltrane group.

The present-day Jones still leads from the rear, as it were, and anyone appraising his status on the strength of current output would be amazed by the ceaseless, coruscating patterns. As a group leader, his promptings demand one hundred per cent concentration of his sidemen.

Carlos N. Ward b. Panama Canal Zone, 1 May 1940

The Ward family settled in Seattle, Washington, in 1953, and the young Carlos could be found in rock and R'n'B bands prior to being drafted in 1962. Back in civilian life he fell into the company of important figures from the explosive 'new thing' of the sixties, including Don Cherry, Sam Rivers and Pharoah Sanders. He then became part of the nucleus of enquiring acolytes learning at the feet of the great John Coltrane, toured with Sunny Murray, played as a member of the *Rashied Ali Quartet* and fitted in the odd gig for reggae and Latin American bands.

Living with the tag of being one of Coltrane's disciples did not hang easily on Ward's shoulders, and many people were not wholly convinced of his qualities as a commanding improviser. Nevertheless, his association with Abdullah Ibrahim brought new respect in the eighties, the superb melodic passages from both alto and flute he pours forth receiving well-deserved praise whether at live gigs or on record. Much of the same can be heard in Don Cherry's band *Nu* where his integration into the group concept is just about perfect.

150

Jean-Baptiste (Illinois) Jacquet   b. Broussard, Louisiana, USA, 31 October 1922

Although born in Louisiana, Jacquet was brought up in Texas and paved his way in the band of Milt Larkins, a stopping-off point for other musicians, such as Arnett Cobb, Eddie 'Cleanhead' Vinson and T-Bone Walker. However, the most important move of his career came when he joined the Lionel Hampton band and recorded the big-selling *Flying Home*, the tenor solo becoming a compulsory part of any future arrangement of the piece. Hampton was required to resurrect the tune as a rousing finale to concerts for many years to come. That was in 1942, and subsequently his spells with Cab Calloway and Count Basie coincided with *Jazz at the Philharmonic* appearances, in addition to his setting up his own groups.

In the sixties and seventies Jacquet trios presented organists Milt Buckner and Wild Bill Davis. The 1967 Newport Jazz Festival found him keeping company with Hampton as he went 'flying home' once again. Frequent touring kept him busy and in 1984 he put together a big band, the *Jazz Legends*.

Jacquet is a tenor-player out of the classic mould, who, having been categorized as a high-note screamer, has had to battle for recognition as a far more sensitive performer, although more than capable of raising the temperature a degree or two.

Arthur (Art) Blakey (Abdullah Ibn Buhaina)   b. Pittsburgh, Pennsylvania, USA,
11 October 1919

Blakey is arguably one of the premier half-dozen drummers in the history of jazz
and must be regarded as one of the founding fathers of modern drumming. He has
inspired many but been surpassed by very few in terms of ability to put fire into a
band.

He was introduced to the drum kit when he was 'told' by a gangster club-owner
that he should vacate the piano stool he occupied to accommodate the
up-and-coming Errol Garner. Present at the inception of be-bop, it was he who
powered the legendary *Billy Eckstine Big Band* in the company of Charlie Parker,
Dizzy Gillespie and Fats Navarro.

His group the *Jazz Messengers* is an indisputable breeding-ground for young
talent. Since the early versions of the band, founded in the 1950s (suitably
documented in a number of albums on the Blue Note label), it has spawned such
influential musicians as Lee Morgan, McCoy Tyner, Wayne Shorter and Freddie
Hubbard. Most recently the phenomenally gifted Wynton Marsalis stepped out of
the group to make a significant contribution to both the jazz and classical worlds.

Blakey remains the most active of leaders, enthusiasm undimmed and packing
the Messengers with accomplished newcomers inevitably destined for the brightest
of futures. In the UK particularly, the hard bop styling of the music has found
popularity with a new generation who regard the drummer as a guru figure.

Robert (Bobby) Hutcherson   b. Los Angeles, California, USA, 27 January 1941

In contemporary terms the vibraharp is regarded as a Cinderella instrument, with few practitioners making a great impact over and above the established figures like Milt Jackson, Terry Gibbs and Lionel Hampton. In the sixties, Gary Burton cultivated a strong following, the excellent Walt Dickerson languished in semi-obscurity, and Bobby Hutcherson entered into the challenging New York world inhabited by Jackie McLean, Hank Mobley, Eric Dolphy and Archie Shepp. The memorable Dolphy recording *Out To Lunch* features the skittering vibes sound of Hutcherson, as do the famous Shepp epics of 1965, *New Thing at Newport* and *On This Night*.

Towards the close of the sixties, Blue Note issued a number of albums graced by Hutcherson's skills but by 1969 he was back on the West Coast co-leading a quintet with tenor-player Harold Land. The following years were a fairly fallow period but in 1982 he visited Britain with the *Timeless All Stars*, returning a year later in an All Star line-up that headlined the Bracknell Jazz Festival, unfortunately lacking the billed Jackie McLean. In 1984 he was in the studio for *Good Bait*, an interesting generation mix with the developing Branford Marsalis and veteran drummer Philly Joe Jones on one of his last dates. Whilst appreciating the percussion implications of the vibraharp, Hutcherson decided that it could be used far more readily as tonal colouration in the ensemble area and gave the instrument a far more free-ranging function, made almost compulsory by the 'new thingers' of the early sixties.

Joseph Goreed (Joe) Williams   b. Cordele, Georgia, USA, 12 December 1918

The urbane and sophisticated Joe Williams has not always met the credentials demanded by a percentage of the jazz fraternity and was positively frowned upon by many Count Basie fans during his stay with the band from 1954 to 1960. There were claims that he didn't swing, and his occasionally mannered delivery infuriated those with fond memories of the far more basic charms of Jimmy Rushing. The truth of the matter was, and still remains, that Joe's stylish tones deserved to be recognized for their own qualities. When he relaxes into his material, particularly at mid-tempo, the phrasing cannot be faulted, the intonation is near perfect, the swing content marked and the charm of the man infectious.

Before joining Basie Williams had already achieved a modicum of popular success with his version of *Every Day I Have the Blues*, recorded with King Kolax. When leaving Basie he retained that popularity, far beyond the reaches of the purists. With the *Harry Edison Quintet* in tow, then the *Junior Mance Trio*, he travelled extensively at home and abroad, achieving somewhat of triumph at Newport '63, the trio strengthened by Coleman Hawkins, Zoot Sims, Howard McGhee and Clark Terry, the ambiance perfect, the crowd loving every minute.

The constant demand for his services continued unabated and reunions with Basie held a very special place in his heart. How nice to see him in London in 1985, interpretive skills intact, sharing the stage with the Count's old band, under the directorship of Thad Jones.

Frederick William (Freddie) Green   b. Charleston, South Carolina, USA, 31 March 1911, d. 1986

Freddie Green was recommended to Count Basie by John Hammond and in 1937 took up position at the heart of one of the most famous rhythm sections in jazz history: Basie himself on piano, Green (guitar), Walter Page (bass) and Jo Jones (drums), the powerhouse for Buck Clayton, Harry Edison, Dicky Wells, Herschel Evans, Lester Young et al. Green eschewed the limelight, happy to supply the rhythmic impetus that others needed.

In 1950 Basie disbanded to form a much smaller grouping and dispensed with the services of the guitarist, who nevertheless soon reappeared in the Basie organization. The big band reassembled two years later, and Green stayed next to the Count until his death in 1984.

In addition to his tireless efforts for the great band-leader, he also took himself into the studio with other Basie sidemen to back Billie Holliday on a number of her very best recordings during the late thirties. Typical of an extremely self-effacing individual, very few records exist under his own name but surely Green has left behind him sufficient proof to ensure his place in all future jazz histories.

Acknowledgements

Peter Gamble acknowledges reference to the following books in preparation of his text:

John Litweiler, *The Freedom Principle* (Blandford, 1985)

Ian Carr, Digby Fairweather, Brian Priestley, *Jazz, The Essential Companion* (Grafton, 1987)

Barry McRae, *The Jazz Handbook* (Longman, 1987)

Jazz on Record (Hanover, 1968)

John Chilton, *Who's Who of Jazz* (Macmillan, 1972)

Leonard Feather and Ira Gitler, *The Encyclopaedia of Jazz in the Seventies* (Quartet, 1978)

David Meeker, *Jazz in the Movies* (Talisman, 1981)

Brian Case, Stan Britt, Chrissie Murray, *The Illustrated Encyclopedia of Jazz* (Salamander, 1986)

Albert McCarthy, *Big Band Jazz* (Peerage, 1983)

Valerie Wilmer, *As Serious As Your Life* (Pluto, 1987)

Also periodicals *Jazz Journal International* (UK), *The Wire* (UK), *Cadence* (USA), *Coda* (Canada).

Peter Symes would like to say a special 'thanks' to Valerie Mills for her continuous encouragement with this book and to fellow-photographers Julian Bell and Randell Webb for their support.